Dagga: A Short History

Dagga: A Short History

(then, now & just now)

Hazel Crampton

JACANA

First published by Jacana Media (Pty) Ltd in 2015

10 Orange Street
Sunnyside
Auckland Park 2092
South Africa
+2711 628 3200
www.jacana.co.za

ISBN 978-1-4314-2215-9

Set in Sabon 11/16pt
Printed and bound by Shumani Mills Communications,
Parow, Cape Town
Job No. 002559

Also available as an e-book:
d-PDF ISBN 978-1-4314-2313-2
ePUB ISBN 978-1-4314-2314-9
mobi file ISBN 978-1-4314-2315-6

See a complete list of Jacana titles at www.jacana.co.za

*I hate people who think it's clever
to take drugs ... like customs officers.*

(Jack Dee: *City Press*, Johannesburg,
29 June 2014; also attributed to Mick Miller:
Jarski 2004: 433)

for
Kash, Ky & Jeremy

with all my love

Contents

Author's note

This book is a conversation piece. My hope is to provide a background to dagga in South Africa and to ignite debate on emerging issues such as licensing, legalisation and taxation. This book is not intended as a comprehensive take on dagga, aka cannabis, marijuana, bhanga, ganga, pot, zol, weed, etc., but as an overview.

My thanks to Maggie Davey and Jeremy Pickering, without whom it would not have been written, Lara Jacob, my editor, and the staff of the Cory Library for Historical Research, Rhodes University, Grahamstown.

When dagga was legal

Researchers have discovered that chocolate
produces some of the same reactions in the
brain as marijuana. The researchers also
discovered some other similarities between the
two but can't remember what they are.
(Matt Lauer: Lloyd & Mitchinson 2009: 92)

Popular perception of marijuana in America is informed largely by the free-wheeling beats and free-loving hippies of the 1950s and 1960s, but its provenance in South Africa, where it is usually called dagga, is altogether more ancient.

The word *dagga* first appears in writing in 1658, in the journal of Jan van Riebeeck, commander of the Cape of Good Hope. Six years earlier, the Dutch had founded a refreshment station, on what is now the site of modern Cape Town, to supply their fleets with fresh water, meat and vegetables on the long voyages to and from the East Indies. On 21 June 1658, Eva, a young member of the indigenous Khoikhoi who acted as Van Riebeeck's interpreter, told him of 'the Hancumqua' who lived further inland 'cultivating the soil in which they grow *daccha*, a dry herb which the [Khoikhoi] chew, which makes them drunk, and which they highly esteem'. These Hancumqua, Van Riebeeck noted, 'make a living by keeping cattle and planting the valuable herb *dacha*, which drugs their brains, just like opium ... and that is why this tribe is so fond of it'.[1]

Thereafter dagga appears regularly throughout the historical record. The Dutchman, Olfert Dapper, in 1668, for example, remarked that it 'affects [the Khoikhoi's] brains and makes them giddy, they behave like crazy and senseless people, performing all sorts of strange gestures and wonderful grimaces'. Willem ten Rhyne in 1673 recorded that dagga 'makes them monstrous drunk'. Ensign Beutler in 1752 met a man on the Sundays River who 'smoked himself silly and behaved like a mad and frenzied person', so much so that 'his friends hereupon hid his bows, arrows and assegais'. The trader George Thompson in 1827 noted that dagga 'speedily intoxicates those who smoke it profusely, sometimes rendering them for a time quite mad'.[2] As late as 1886, on the orders of the Resident Magistrate, the bug-infested jail at Springbok, Namaqualand, was fumigated by means of copious amounts of dagga-smoke.[3]

At the time such texts elicited little comment. But in modern reprints the very same texts provoked a very

Kolbe's illustration of 1719 is possibly the earliest drawing of the plant which 'the Hottentots [Khoikhoi] cal'd *Dacha*'.[4]

different response. Their modern editors reacted with determined denialism and, in a flurry of footnotes, furiously declared that the dagga referred to was not *Cannabis sativa* (marijuana), but *Leonotis leonurus*, a rather innocuous weed also known as 'wild hemp'.[5]

Why, one wonders? It is difficult to see how the two could have been confused as they're clearly different to the naked eye.

Cannabis sativa has a distinctive, five-fingered leaf, which can be clearly seen in Kolbe's drawing of 1719 (see page 24). This five-fingered leaf is entirely absent in *Leonotis leonurus,* which has, instead, bright sprays of orange flowers.

Nor are the differences purely aesthetic. *Cannabis sativa* is a powerful narcotic: 'a Phantastica, a hallucinogenic drug that causes mental exhilaration and nervous excitation'.[6] Euphoria is dagga's most notable effect; the drug induces a sense of well-being often accompanied by the giggles. Early writers such as Kolbe concur: dagga 'is a Thing, of which the Hottentots are ... likewise mighty fond. It banishes Care and Anxiety, say they, like Wine or Brandy, and inspires them with a Million of Delightful Fancies'.[7]

Whatever the Khoi were imbibing caused very strong reactions, ranging from 'drunk' to giddy and silly. *Leonotis leonurus*, by comparison, has a much milder effect – it's simply not in the same league as dagga. Anti-dagga campaigners concur: 'Leonotis is not the plant which is smoked in South Africa for its hedonistic pleasure'.[8]

Perhaps the fact that most of these modern editors – and we're talking about very learned men here, of the stature and erudition of Professor Forbes, Professor Kirby and Dr Mossop – were middle-aged, middle-class, white men of the mid-twentieth century had something to do with their confusion. Born too early, they wouldn't have known the Summer of Love from winter in the Antarctic.

They simply couldn't see the wood for the *boom*.[9]

Another and more probable reason, though, is that dagga – *Cannabis sativa* – is illegal in South Africa. *Leonotis leonurus* is not.

Cannabis sativa is:

Leonotis leonurus is:

In other words, a sense of decorum may also have been to blame.

It wasn't like that to begin with. During the first centuries of colonial settlement, dagga was a perfectly legal substance. Eminent travellers and officials, farmers and even missionaries paid their servants and guides with dagga, or bartered the drug for cattle and services. Some grew it specifically for that purpose. The missionaries at Klaarwater, now Griquatown, raised dagga in their church gardens to trade with the neighbouring San or Bushmen.[10] When the trader George Thompson stopped over at a Boer farmhouse north of Graaff-Reinet in 1823, he found a large quantity of dagga hanging, drying, from the rafters. Thompson claimed that the Boers 'seldom use the *dacha* themselves'. But this is not borne out by independent evidence.[11]

The very serious *Volksgeneeskuns in Suid-Afrika: 'n Kultuur-historiese oorsig, benewens 'n uitgebreide versameling Boererate*, published by *Die Suid-Afrikaanse Akademie vir Wetenskap en Kuns* in about 1965, lists 89 Afrikaner home-remedies that utilised dagga. And while some, such as *klipdagga, wildedagga* or *knopdagga*, may refer to *Leonotis* or *Leonotis leonurus*, at least 25 of the recipes insist on the use of real dagga, in other words *Cannabis sativa*. Dagga leaf tea, for example, was widely used to reduce high blood pressure. Dagga smoke stopped bleeding. Dagga was also used in treating poisonous bites. And so on.

Dagga was not only a favourite among the *plattelandse tannies* and their home-remedies. According to Professor Ellison Kahn, dagga smoking was 'a way of life' among the old *trekboers* and was fairly widely enjoyed as a sundowner as late as the First World War. It was 'sold freely over the counter'. It was even advertised in the press.[12]

But by the early twentieth century things had begun to change.

In 1903 the Orange River Colony passed the

Dagga Prohibition Ordinance Act 43, whereby the sale of dagga became an offence. Use and possession remained legal, but in 1922 the Customs and Excise Duties Amendment Act 35 prohibited in general the importation, conveyance, sale and supply, as well as the use and possession of dagga and other habit-forming drugs. Six years later, in 1928, dagga's cultivation too was made illegal. In a paper on Khoikhoi medicine published immediately afterwards, in December 1928, the writer, P. W. Laidler, recognises only two species of dagga: *wildedagga* and *klipdagga*, both species of *Leonotis*.[13] *Cannabis sativa* isn't mentioned. It is as if it had been deliberately obliterated from the record – and probably was.

With the promulgation of the Medical, Dental and Pharmacy Act 13 of 1928 the criminalisation of dagga was complete. Moreover, it gave the magistrates' courts very extensive powers of punishment for any offences under the said Act.[14] Waiting in the wings, however, was an even tougher Act, the Abuse of Dependence-producing Substances and Rehabilitation Centres Act 41 of 1971, which would not only increase the punitive jurisdiction of these courts but carried extremely harsh minimum sentences.

Although the dreaded 'Drugs Act', as it would become known, was still a long way off, by the mid-twentieth century when the above-mentioned respected and respectable historians were at the height of their careers, dagga had already been illegal – and heavily stigmatised – for many decades. For them, editing the old missionaries' and explorers' journals, in which dagga-dealing was openly admitted, must have been severely embarrassing. Rather than admitting that our founding fathers were dope-pushers, it was both easier and more convenient to pretend that the dagga concerned was not *Cannabis sativa*, but *Leonotis leonurus*.

What these historians overlooked, however, was that it was *precisely because* of its narcotic effect that dagga was so sought-after – that, in Van Riebeeck's words, it was more precious to the Khoikhoi than gold was to Europeans. It was *because* it 'drugs the brains' that the Khoikhoi – and so many others – were 'so fond of it'.[15] If the scholars could not tell the two apart, dagga users certainly could. In 1935, 1 123 samples of dagga taken from convicted persons were examined under the auspices of the Secretary for Health at various research centres throughout South Africa. Without exception, all were found to be *Cannabis sativa*.[16]

2

Wheelers & dealers

When I'm good, I'm very, very good, but
when I'm bad, I'm better.

(Mae West: Sherrin 1996: 341)

Humans have always been predisposed towards mood-altering substances. As someone once said: 'Man, being reasonable, must get drunk.' Since the beginning of time we have brewed, chewed, fermented, distilled, smoked and sniffed a variety of grains, leaves, fruits, vegetables, and whatever else we can, in order to lower our inhibitions, reduce our stress, enhance our experiences and heighten or dull our emotions, mostly in the hope of lightening our hearts, but perhaps as often just lightening our wallets and burdening ourselves with remorse. Humans seem to have recognised the narcotic qualities of dagga, in particular, very early on and for the last 6 000 years or so its spread has been associated with human settlements.[17]

In southern Africa about the only people who seem to have abstained, and then only briefly, were the Tlhaping from around present-day Kuruman, whose king, Matibe, tried to discourage its use in the 1820s. (His disaffection may have been due to some kind of narcotic psychosis brought on by an overdose, as he is said to have 'got sick' from smoking too much dagga.[18]) Otherwise, throughout the subcontinent, from the coastal settlements of Mozambique to the deep interior, everyone in southern Africa used dagga, including the Khoi, the San, the Sotho-Tswana and Nguni. The Shona of Zimbabwe also used it. At least two of the kings of the famed gold-trading empire of Monomotapa, for example, were chronic users, one being Mupunzagutu, who is thought to have ruled in the mid-eighteenth century.

Mupunzagutu 'used to smoke dagga (mbanje) a lot and was given the nickname *Nyakudja-mbanje*', or 'Marijuana-Eater'. Like modern potheads the world over, he fancied himself as a bit of a musician and spent hours composing tunes on the marimba:

> His favourite tune, which is still played today, is called 'Rumbo rwaMupunzagutu'. It runs as follows: *Imbopa, Imbopa, uchipire mwana anokanza musango* (Give a scrap, just a scrap for the child who roots for some food in the bundu).[19]

Now, does that sound like *Cannabis sativa* or not?

As mentioned above, *Cannabis sativa* and *leonotis* are quite distinct from one another. They're physically different and their psychoactive effects are different. They also have different origins, in so far as the former is exotic and the latter not. Although it grows like a weed here, *Cannabis sativa* is not indigenous to southern Africa. Originally native to Central Asia, it was its narcotic qualities that ensured its rapid spread elsewhere. As early as 4000 BC it had reached China and by 1500 to 1000 BC it had reached India. According to Vedic accounts (early Hindu religious texts written in Sanskrit), dagga was created when the gods 'stirred the heavenly oceans with the peak of Mount Mandara', possibly Mount Everest, and a drop of the celestial nectar fell to earth, whence sprang a sacred plant. It became the favourite plant of Indra, Lord of Lords, and was subsequently brought down from the Himalayas by the god Shiva for the 'use and enjoyment' of humankind.[20] Dagga was revered by the Buddhists too, whose legendary Prince Siddharta is said to have subsisted on an exclusive diet of dagga seeds for six years, in search of enlightenment[21] – the slow pace of which may have due to the fact that he limited himself to just one seed a day. Dagga's later spread has been linked to the expansion of Islam, and especially to that of the mystical Sufis, sometimes described as the 'hippies of the Arab world'.[22]

In Van Riebeeck's day, the Khoikhoi of the south-

'Dgauas Land' is clearly visible on this detail of Wentzel's large map of 1752, the eastern Cape portion of which is the earliest known cartographical record of the region.[23]

western Cape obtained their dagga from cultivators further east, including the Hessequa and Hancumqua who lived between modern Swellendam and Mossel Bay. Other peoples to the north-east, the Chamaquas, Omaquas, Atiquas, Houtunquas, and Cauquas, also grew dagga.[24] Judging by its name, Daggaboersnek ('Dagga-farmers pass') near Cradock seems likely to have been one of the more popular localities.

Many of these early dagga-farmers traded dagga with others further afield. According to shipwreck survivors, the south-western Khoikhoi took dagga to the Xhosa on annual trading trips.

It is a trade that is still flourishing hundreds of years later, despite its illegality. Every day people travel between the western and eastern Cape trafficking in dagga. It is transported by the sack-full in vehicles ranging from the flashy to the faulty, in taxis, *bakkies* and the boots of cars.[25] They travel at night and by day, ferrying the weed from the plots and plantations of the eastern Cape to the flesh-pots and bottle-necks of Cape Town.

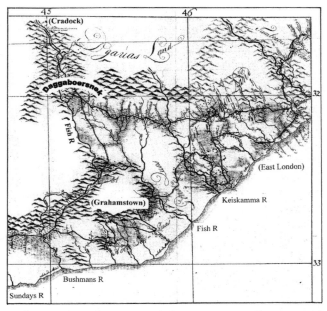

Wider, annotated version of the same map of 1752, with modern town-names in brackets, showing 'Dgauas Land' in the Daggaboersnek region, just south of modern Cradock.[26]

Dagga also thrived on the myriad islands in the Orange/Gariep River above Augrabies Falls. And it packed quite a punch – Hendrik Wikar who visited the islands in the late 1700s says those who smoked it became so 'drunk' that some lost consciousness and fell into the fire, before being rescued by their friends.[27]

Some historians have claimed that dagga was introduced to the Cape by the Dutch. But they're wrong: there is ample evidence that its arrival long preceded that of the Europeans. Two pipes used for

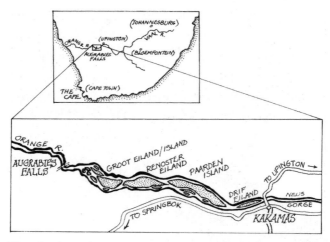

The islands on the Orange River, above Augrabies Falls, where dagga once 'grew most luxuriantly'.[28]

smoking *I'daha* were among artefacts recovered at Great Zimbabwe, which dates back to around 1250 AD. One early writer maintains that dagga has been used in southern Africa 'from time immemorial', an unfortunate phrase perhaps since dagga-users aren't known for their longevity of recall.[29]

Cannabis sativa is believed to have been introduced to southern Africa around a thousand years ago by Asian traders, who used the monsoons to carry them across the Indian Ocean. These are seasonal winds which blow in one direction for part of the year and the other way for another part of the year, facilitating a trade that was mutually profitable and very ancient.

The drug was one of the earliest trade items in a prehistoric trade network which extended deep into the subcontinent from the shores of the Indian Ocean. The earliest surviving written documentation of east Africa's trade with India and Arabia dates back to about 76 AD, and the earliest and southern-most Muslim trading settlement that has been found to date is at Chibuene, a few kilometres south of Vilanculo, on the Mozambican mainland opposite the Bazaruto archipelago. A Muslim grave has been excavated at Chibuene dating back to about 850 AD. This is exactly contemporaneous with Arab trade with Schroda near Mapungubwe, some thousand kilometres up the Limpopo River.[30]

Dagga's point of entry was the Mozambique coast. We know this because of its linguistic trail. The Sanskrit word for dagga is *bhanga;* in Hindi it is called *bhang.* From the thirteenth century on, it appears in Islamic writings as *banj.* This was the word by which it first became known in southern Africa, and by variations of which it is still known to the peoples in the north-east of the country – closest to the Mozambique coast. Among the Tonga of the Zambezi Valley, for example, it is called *mbange;* among the Shona *mbanji,* among the Tsonga of southern Mozambique *mbangi,* and among the Venda *mbanzhe.*[31]

Quite how the Khoi came to call it *dagga* is uncertain. According to the *Suid-Afrikaanse Akademie vir Wetenskap en Kuns* the word 'was taken over from the Hottentots' and is 'undoubtedly ... one of the earliest loan words in Afrikaans'.[32]

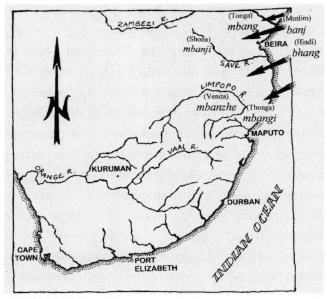

Bhang's *linguistic trail.*

Burchell in 1812 claimed that dagga was a Khoisan corruption of the Dutch greeting *dag!*, meaning 'good day'. But, as mentioned above, it was already known as *dacha* when the first Dutch arrived at the Cape. Smith, in his *Common South African Plants*, also believed it was originally a Khoi word: *dacha(b)*. The linguist Carl Meinhof has suggested the word is a corruption of the Arabic term *duXan*, meaning 'tobacco'. The late arrival of tobacco – with the Portuguese in the early 1500s – mitigates against this though. Another possibility is that the term dagga was derived from *maqhah*, an Arabic word meaning 'a gathering, or

16

café', since the smoking of dagga-pipes was very much a communal activity.[33]

The most popular method of smoking dagga in southern Africa in earlier times was the *hookah* – the Arabs' and Indians' preferred method of smoking, the *huqqah,* or water-pipe. Hookahs were in use long before the spread of tobacco in the sixteenth and seventeenth centuries. They originated in north-western India over a thousand years ago, and were used for smoking opium and hashish.

The water cools the smoke and makes it less irritating to the throat, and Africanised hookahs were widely used. The Tsonga of southern Mozambique made their hookahs from animal horn. Many others did too. The Xhosa of the eastern Cape in 1801 used water-pipes of ox horn. So did the Zulus. The Rolong near modern Mahikeng smoked hookahs of gemsbok horn, the Khoikhoi of the present Humansdorp area used hookahs of eland-horn. The San or Bushmen of the Tarka district of the eighteenth century referred to dagga as *xubhuxubhu,* meaning 'gurgling liquid', an onomatopoeic term which almost certainly referred to the water-pipe.[34] In Saudi Arabia, the hookah is also known by an onomatopoeic name, the *hubble-bubble,* but the San word bears a startling similarity to the Assyrian word for dagga (*qunubu,* from *qunnabu,* meaning 'noise'), not to mention that the Hebrew (*qanneb*), Persian (*quonnab*) and even Celtic (*quannab*) are words for the same.[35]

Tsonga hookah-smoker, 1798.[36]

Among the first southern Africans to experiment with the hookah were probably the Tsonga around Maputo, in southern Mozambique, and they adopted it wholeheartedly. According to a visitor in the 1820s they considered the 'hubble-bubble' one of 'the greatest luxuries of life'.[37]

The pipe consisted of a reed with a small pierced

wooden or stone bowl on its upper extremity. The lower extremity of the reed was attached to a horn half-filled with water. The dagga was placed in the bowl and lit. With one hand, the smoker closed the horn, leaving a narrow opening through which he sucked vigorously, to form a vacuum. The smoke was drawn through the reed whence it bubbled through the water, cooling it, and then into the mouth of the smoker.

Hookahs may cool the smoke but they produce far more of it, delivering about eight times more carbon dioxide and about 36 times more tar than a normal cigarette.[38] Smoking dagga through a hookah also delivers far more tetrahydrocannabinol (THC, the psychotropic principle of dagga) than the average joint, which means the smoker gets stoned faster. The smoke also causes excessive salivation and when stoned the Tsonga dagga-smoker's favourite game was a saliva fight. Using a hollow reed they began to fight by blowing spit through it on the ground. The simplest form of the game consisted in squirting as long a stream of saliva as possible: 'He who squirts the furtherest, wins.'[39]

There was also a more complicated game, so complicated that the missionary-anthropologist Henri Junod needed a diagram to explain it.

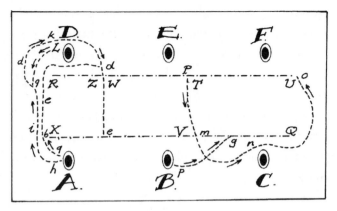

Saliva contest of Tsonga dagga smokers.[40]

The game went something like this:

There are two sides, each with his pipe. Three men, A. B. C. oppose three others, D. E. F. First of all, each side protects itself by making a saliva fence, line X. Q. for the first side, R. U. for the second one. Unhappily for D. E. F. the saliva dries up on the point Z. W. and so their fence is broken. A. takes his advantages. He begins to squirt out his saliva on the line *a, b, c, d...*, passes through the opening Z. W., and, having come back victoriously to *e*, he has destroyed all the fortifications R. Z. Suppose D. wants to protect himself. He tries to close the access to his position by drawing the line *f, g*. But, arrived in *g*, he comes to the end of his saliva (a helela), and A. who started in *h*, having arrived in *i*, turns round the point *g*, where his enemy has miserably stopped, and, going on, *j*, *k*, reaches the opening *d.* and triumphantly ends his campaign in *e*!

But E. of the opposite camp has noticed a gate in the barrier X. Q. The saliva has dried there. He quickly carries his blow-pipe across the battle field, squirting all the time, passes through the opening Y. He draws the line *l*, *m*, *n*, *o* and so destroys the part Q. Y. of the fortification X. Q. Should B. be quick enough, he might prevent him accomplishing his plan by drawing the line *p. q*... And so on! [41]

All of which sounds rather as though Junod had smoked a couple of pipes himself.

3

A slippery slope: The criminalisation of dagga

[Dagga] is truly an unpredictable drug used by unpredictable people and with unpredictable consequences.

(A.D. Bensusan: Bensusan 1972: 123)

Dagga is believed to be one of the world's earliest cultivated plants. Its generic name, *Cannabis sativa*, bestowed in 1753 by Linnaeus, the 'father of botany', may be translated as '*cultivated* cannabis'. It is a plant synonymous with human habitation, and it owes its distribution across the world almost exclusively to human agency.

Dagga is a member of the hemp family, a fibrous, botanically versatile plant able to adapt to such a variety of different climates and conditions that it is one of the most widely distributed plants in the world, found from India to south and central America, from the Caribbean to southern Africa, and from Mongolia to southern Britain – and that, as one commentator notes, 'is just in the open, not under glass'. Its popularity is closely bound up with both its production of fibre, used in the manufacture of rope, paper and fabric, and its psychoactive properties. The oldest Chinese treatise on agriculture, the *Xia Xiao Zheng* written in the sixteenth century BC, lists hemp as an important crop. But dagga is also a muscle-relaxing, euphoric intoxicant. Its active ingredient, the phenol compound tetrahydrocannabinol, or THC, is most often concentrated in the female flowers, and cultivators understood the importance of differentiating male from female hemp, or *ma*, from a very early date. The earliest Chinese dictionary, for example, clearly distinguishes male from female plants as *xi ma* and *ju ma* respectively.[42] (Any similarity between *ju ma* and *jou ma* is, presumably, purely coincidental.)

Dagga is an annual, the growth cycle of which consists of two stages, a vegetative stage followed by a flowering stage, where-after the plant dies. Each stage displays a distinctive leaf arrangement. In its vegetative state, the leaves grow in opposing pairs along the main stem. With the onset of flowering the plant bifurcates at the base of each leaf, and on each of these branches the leaves alternate, no longer growing opposite one another.[43]

The distinctive five-fingered leaf of the dagga plant, Cannabis sativa.

Typically dagga remains in its vegetative state during the summer months and only begins flowering with the onset of winter and its shorter periods of daylight. It is then that the plant is at its most potent, with the THC concentrated in the female flower buds.[44]

Quantifying and qualifying the effects of THC is a bit of a conundrum. The name *marijuana* is a Spanish corruption of the Portuguese word *marihuana*, meaning 'intoxicated'. But different varieties of dagga have different levels of potency, and depend on many factors, not least those relating to the growth, picking and storage of the plant. In the 1970s a South African doctor, A.D. Bensusan, identified three main grades of

The chemical structure of THC, the active ingredient of dagga.[45]

potency, which he listed in descending order. Uppermost was what he termed hashish, prepared from resin taken from the tops of mature female plants, in which the THC is usually concentrated. Then came ganga, an intermediate grade taken from the flowering tops and selected leaves, and lastly 'marihuana', a mixture of dried leaves, stems and seeds. Recent research has shown he wasn't far off the mark: hashish-oil has a THC content as high as 85 per cent, hashish of 20 per cent and dagga leaves from just 5–10 per cent.[46]

Dagga's effects may also vary according to how it is consumed. Besides smoking it, dagga can be drunk as a tea, made from boiling the leaves in water. It can also be eaten, added to flour to produce dagga cookies or sweet cakes, or added to curries and other savoury foods. The earliest Cape records show that the Khoikhoi may have done them all. Back in 1668, for example, the Hessequa who lived around modern Swellendam mixed their dagga with water and drank it 'to become drunk'. They also made dagga cookies: in 1686, in what may be the first written record of the great south Africanism 'braai', Ten Rhyne wrote that the southern Khoi 'bray' their dagga carefully, 'and after braying, make it into balls and eat it, as many Mahomedans do with Amsion or opium', which made them 'monstrous drunk'.[47] They knew what they were doing: when dagga is eaten its psychoactive effect is much stronger and lasts much longer than when it is smoked.[48]

The effects of dagga vary widely not only according to the method of consumption but also from individual to individual. It may also affect the same individual differently at different times and under different conditions. In the words of one of dagga's detractors, 'calm and mild delirium may result in apathetic people; imaginative personalities may experience brilliant and varied hallucinations; savage reactions such as mad rage may be precipitated in a human brute.'[49] And herein lies the rub.

It is probably no coincidence that the demonisation of dagga in South Africa began at a time of increasing racial discrimination and rising Afrikaner nationalism. Criminalising dagga was all part of digging a deeper ditch between South Africans of different backgrounds and cultures. Paterson, in a recent dissertation on prohibition and resistance, came to the same conclusion: 'the colonial construction of personhood, which later provided the foundation for apartheid policy, also provided the foundation for the prohibition of cannabis.'[50]

Fear, racism and political ideology were all part of the brew: the conceit that dagga exaggerated innate character traits was intertwined with racial prejudice, bolstered by corrupted notions of Darwinism. Colonialism was founded on a hierarchy of colour, a kind of social pyramid with a broad base of darker humanity, lightening incrementally as the pyramid narrowed towards its apex. Unsurprisingly, it was precisely those who enjoyed the rarefied air and privileges at the top, who were its most fervent enforcers – the white guys.

Those at the bottom – the black guys – were considered 'more primitive' than the former, and from there it was just a short conceptual leap to 'more savage' and 'more disposed to criminality', the general idea being that 'if criminals were like savages, then all savages were potential criminals'.[51]

The 'debate', if it can be called that, which preceded the introduction of the Abuse of Dependence-producing Substances and Rehabilitation Centres Act 41 of 1971 (the so-called 'Drugs Act'), included these and all sorts of other bogies, including the fear of 'escalation' – that the use of dagga would inevitably lead to harder, more dangerous drugs. Such claims had long been challenged, even before the advent of the Drugs Act. In 1970, for example, John Kaplan, Professor of Law at Stanford University, noted that it was only when cannabis became unavailable that some users, and only some, turned to more dangerous drugs. Yet, as late as 2014 online junkies continued to maintain that 'Dagga is the big problem that all druggies start with!' Kaplan, incidentally, also suggested that alcohol is more likely to lead to violent crime than dagga, a finding supported a year later by the World Health Organization report of November 1971, which showed that juvenile dagga users 'were less likely to show aggressive behaviour than juveniles who preferred alcohol'.[52]

Other colonial fears concerned indolence. Workers were expected to work but dagga, according to an 1887 Commission, caused 'unsteadiness in the performance of work' and an 'incapacity for exertion'. Overlooking other probable causes of worker apathy, such as poor nutrition, poor medical care and poor living conditions, the Commission strongly recommended that the use and sale of dagga be prohibited. Not all agreed. In 1908 when mine managers were petitioned to stop the mine stores from selling dagga to African workers, they declined; dagga was not used in excess, the managers argued, and actually seemed to make the miners more productive. Perhaps not coincidentally, there is evidence of commercial, white-owned farms supplying dagga to the mines during this period, some from as far away as the southern Cape.[53]

Another fear was that dagga lowered self-control and simultaneously 'inflamed the passions'. There was also concern that whites who used dagga set 'a bad example' to blacks,[54] as well as the fear that dagga users were more likely to breach the barriers between racial groups, and that contact between such groups could cause the degeneration of those individuals belonging to the 'higher order' in the established hierarchy.[55] Sex was pretty high on the list. So was the fear of crime.

This included what may be termed mad crime, violent crime and even just-plain-*dof* crime. Medical men were adamant that 'the continued use of dagga leads to an increasing mental dullness and moral deterioration which sooner or later causes its user to resort to crime'. Under the influence of dagga, Dr Bensusan claimed, the danger of 'committing premeditated murder is very great; it can happen in cold blood, without any reason or motive, unexpectedly, without any preceding quarrel; often the murderer does not even know the victim and kills simply for pleasure'. Bensusan considered eating dagga to be particularly dangerous: 'Occasionally Africans eat the raw leaves and several cases have occurred in which they exhibited almost superhuman energy and power after partaking in this way – an African was able to brush aside eight policemen and he fought them off for some time before they were able to overpower him.'[56]

All these claims were based on what their proponents liked to term a 'scientific basis', but few were able to provide empirical data to back them up. It was a Catch-22 situation: because dagga was illegal in South

Africa, research was severely curtailed if not actually *verboten*; there were certainly no human studies nor scientific trials, and since dagga was scientifically so little understood, it remained feared and illegal, which meant research was severely curtailed.

About the only thorough investigation into dagga, *The Marihuana Problem in New York* commissioned by the mayor of New York, Fiorello LaGuardia, and published in 1944, was ignored. But then it didn't really fit the South African political agenda – the mayor's report had found that dagga was not addictive and caused 'no mental or physical deterioration'. Modern studies concur. There is also no basis for believing that dagga causes violent or aggressive behaviour. The drug's most common effect is a sense of well-being. It was for this reason that women's temperance societies in the United States in the nineteenth century often advocated the use of dagga in place of alcohol, experience having shown that while drunks often hit their wives, dagga users did not.[57]

As apartheid became more entrenched, the South African establishment became increasingly concerned that dagga fuelled political discontent and protest: across the world, warned one commentator, 'fringe groups' were 'clamouring' for dagga's legalisation. For 'unpredictable people', in other words, it was a small step from breaking the dagga laws to breaking apartheid laws and challenging the 'legality' of the all-white government.[58]

In 1952, the government released an Inter-departmental Committee Report on the Abuse of Dagga, which, like South African society itself, was carefully segregated. The various racial groups and their attitudes to dagga were separately dealt with, in ascending order of 'civilisation'.

If it weren't so tragic it would be hilarious. But the government took it all very seriously. At the bottom were the 'Natives' who, according to the report, saw nothing reprehensible about smoking dagga and did so frequently. Next came the 'Coloureds', who recognised dagga as 'backward' and considered those who used it as lacking in respectability, as did the 'Asiatics' who associated dagga with 'the poorer classes' and looked down on those who used it. At the top were the 'Europeans', who hardly ever used dagga, at least not those 'who are, or wish to be thought respectable'.[59] Dagga, in other words, was the domain of the underclass, consisting mainly of rural blacks, with a few 'others' and a couple of poor whites also slipping through the net.

All that changed with the rise of the so-called hippies in the 1960s and 1970s, and the simultaneous increase in dagga use in South Africa among white, middle-class kids. And it all coincided with the rise of other forms of white, middle-class rebellion and resistance, among them the anti-apartheid movement. It was not only the perceived 'deadliness' in dagga itself that made it so dangerous in the eyes of the establishment, but its ideological dangers.

Pure chemically, dagga has a low toxicity, the lowest of all commonly used intoxicants. But there is no doubt that dagga can aggravate and, some have claimed, perhaps even precipitate psychotic disorders. Research published in the *Lancet* medical journal in 1987, for example, linked dagga use to higher than average rates of psychotic conditions such as schizophrenia.[60] The issue of whether or not dagga actually *caused* schizophrenia was not, however, addressed, and recent research has shown that the only 'link' may be the fact that people who suffer psychotic illness are far more likely to use dagga than the general population.[61]

In 1997, a British study of 1 333 young dagga users reported numerous positive effects of the drug, including stress relief, personal insight, a sharper sense of humour and feelings of euphoria. A number of the respondents, however, also experienced negative symptoms. These included memory impairment (6.1 per cent), demotivation/apathy (4.8 per cent) and paranoia (5.6 per cent).[62]

Subsequent studies have confirmed that acute dagga intoxication does impair memory. A causal link between demotivation and dagga is less certain; some studies have presented data supporting a link, while others have not. ('Negative' studies have been criticised for using subjects from the lower socio-economic spectrum, such as unskilled or partly skilled workers

– as opposed to university students in the 'positive' studies, for example. It has been suggested that the former's amotivation may be less attributable to the dagga consumed than to personality types predisposed to depression, boredom or lack of motivation[63] and, perhaps, dull and inescapable lives.) The links between dagga and paranoia, too, remain subject to ongoing research.

As noted above, different people, in different situations, have different responses to dagga. But there is no doubt that in high doses tetrahydrocannabinol or THC can induce anxiety, panic attacks or paranoia.[64] Especially, perhaps, when the THC comes from South African dagga.

Not all cannabis is the same.[65] The cannabis or hemp smoked in Europe and America, for example, is high in levels of Cannabidiol, or CBD, a non-psychotropic cannabinoid which blocks THC-induced feelings of anxiety. South African dagga, by contrast, contains very low levels of CBD and may cause higher than average levels of anxiety in certain individuals than, say, European cannabis, especially in high doses.[66] Dagga-induced paranoia may even have been to blame for some of the first bad blood between Europeans and indigenous South Africans, at one of the very first meetings between the two.

In November 1497 on his pioneer voyage to the East, the Portuguese mariner Vasco da Gama put in at St Helena Bay, just north of modern Cape Town.

He found the local Khoikhoi keen to trade, and over the next few days, little bells and glass beads were amicably exchanged for animal skins and shells. This happy scene came to an abrupt end when the Khoi gave 'some of the roots of a plant which they eat' to a Portuguese sailor named Fernâo Veloso who shortly thereafter, while making his way back to his ship, began hollering in such an alarming fashion as to bring both his shipmates and the Khoikhoi running. In the confusion a fight broke out, followed by some bloodletting and the hurried departure of the Portuguese.[67]

There's no concrete proof that it was dagga that Veloso had consumed, but his paranoia and the fact that in later European writings dagga is often described as 'a root'[68] suggests it may well have been, especially since dagga-induced anxiety seems to affect inexperienced users most.[69]

Dagga can also damage one's physical health. Dagga smoke contains twice the levels of carcinogens as tobacco smoke, and the bloodstream of a chronic dagga smoker may have as much as five times the carbon monoxide of a chronic cigarette smoker. Exacerbating the problem is the fact that dagga is usually smoked without a filter and mixed with tobacco – and tobacco smokers are 15 to 30 times more likely to get lung cancer than non-smokers. Sometimes dagga is mixed with even more dangerous substances such as mandrax. And while dagga itself is not habit-forming, tobacco and mandrax are *highly*

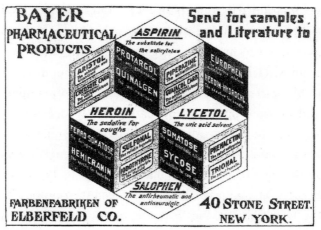

Free samples: an early advertisement for heroin.[70]

addictive. Statistics are not available for the damage caused by the latter, but according to the World Health Organization, tobacco is the world's largest public health hazard, responsible for the deaths of almost six million people every year.[71]

Dagga is known, too, to aggravate existing medical conditions. Researchers at the Beth Israel Medical Centre in Boston, Massachusetts, in 2000, for example, noted a strong correlation between dagga intoxication and the likelihood of a heart attack, brought on by dagga's dramatic increase in heart-rate and blood pressure.[72]

Yet, prior to the First World War, there was no moral stigma attached to dagga, nor for that matter, to other drugs. Coca-Cola contained cocaine.[73] Heroin was marketed as a 'hero' drug. Sherlock Holmes used a 7 per cent solution of cocaine, and Queen Victoria is believed to have used dagga to alleviate menstrual cramps. Her doctor, Sir John Reynolds, found dagga ideal for treating uterine bleeding, migraines, neuralgia and choroid spasms, and categorically declared it 'one of the most valuable medicines we possess'.[74] Even Shakespeare, who, in one of his sonnets refers to the 'noted weed', may have smoked it. Professor Francis Thackeray, Chair of Palaeoanthropology at the University of the Witwatersrand, has examined 24 small pipes found buried in Stratford-upon-Avon, including the Bard's own garden, and found traces of dagga on eight of them.[75] Countless other writers and artists, including Pushkin, Coleridge, Goethe and Byron, dabbled in anything from opium and morphine to hallucinogenic fungi.[76] When Alice, in Lewis Carroll's *Adventures in Wonderland*, peers up over the edge of the mushroom, and comes eyeball to eyeball with 'a large blue caterpillar, that was sitting on the top with its arms folded, quietly smoking a long hookah, and taking not the slightest notice of her or anything else', you can be sure it wasn't tobacco it was smoking.

4

Here be dragons: The law

> *Guns are always the best method for a private*
> *suicide. They are more stylish looking than*
> *single-edged razor blades and natural gas has*
> *got so expensive. Drugs are too chancy. You*
> *may miscalculate the dosage and just have a*
> *good time.*
>
> (P. J. O'ROUKE: SHERRIN 1996: 94)

In December 1971, South Africa's notorious Drugs
Act, the Abuse of Dependence-producing Substances
and Rehabilitation Centres Act 41 of 1971, came into
operation. The Bill passed quickly through the (all-
white) House of Assembly, the formal, first reading
taking place on 4 May, the critical second reading
on 5 and 6 May, the committee stage on 7 May, the
report stage and final reading on 10 May and the
consideration of Senate amendments on 12 May. It
was, says Professor Ellison Kahn:

a piece of legislation that aroused considerable misgivings as regards its punitive aspects among not only certain members of the public who, aware of the gravity of the problem of dependence-forming drugs, nevertheless felt that it went too far in its invasion of the liberty of the citizens and traditional processes of the criminal law; but also among professional legal bodies.[77]

The General Council of the Bar of South Africa sought an interview with the then Prime Minister, John Vorster, to discuss 'the necessity of retaining the fundamental principles of South African jurisprudence even in this type of legislation'. The Council was extremely concerned not only by the legal implications of certain sections of the Act, but also by the fact that it was introduced without prior consultation with the legal profession.[78]

The Council's pleas fell on deaf ears. Which – given that this all took place at the height of apartheid, whose architects and enforcers had little regard for any principles other than their own – is perhaps not surprising. This was, after all, the same government whose Minister of Education in years to come would say of Nelson Mandela: 'You could almost say that for practical purposes he has been set free. He must just reside (in prison) a little longer.'[79]

And so the Drugs Act came into force. This despite the fact that, as a certain Jaap Boekkooi pointed out in a contemporary article, there was a time when dagga was 'as traditionally South African as biltong, boerbeskuit and witblits. Moreover, it was legal stuff through seven-eighths of South Africa's history and sold freely over the counter'. In fact:

> if the Drugs Act had been on the Statute Book a century ago, half the population would have served at least a two-year stretch in gaol, and many a country storekeeper would have been imprisoned for up to 25 years.[80]

The Drugs Act was aimed at preventing non-medicinal use of psychotropic drugs – mood- or mind-altering substances. These fell into three main categories: 'potentially dangerous dependence-producing drugs', such as barbiturates; 'dangerous dependence-producing drugs', including cocaine, morphine and opium; and 'prohibited dependence-producing drugs'. The latter 'have no medicinal value', according to the Act, and included dagga as well as heroin.[81] For our purposes we will refer here only to this third group and only to dagga.

Under the Act it was an offence to use, possess or deal in dagga, or hashish or any plant from which it may be manufactured. The penalties for doing so were harsh, and the sentences mandatory, without the option of a fine. A first conviction for the possession or use of dagga, for example, carried a mandatory prison sentence from two to ten years, a second or subsequent conviction of five to 15 years. A first conviction for dealing in dagga carried a mandatory prison sentence of from five to 15 years and a second or subsequent conviction of ten to 25 years.[82]

Normally the onus is on the State to prove the guilt of the accused. Not with the Drugs Act.

The Act contained a number of presumptions which 'substantially eased the ordinary burden of proof upon the State', in that, unless the accused could prove otherwise, he or she was presumed to have dealt in dagga.[83] For example, anyone found in possession of dagga in excess of 4 ounces, or 115 grams, was presumed to be a dealer. Anyone associated with dagga or found in its vicinity was presumed guilty, even if they were simply a passenger on the same bus where dagga was found; or if they were the manager of a venue who, suspecting that others on the premises might be in possession of dagga, failed to report these suspicions to the police. A first conviction in the latter case carried a mandatory prison sentence of from five to 15 years and a second or subsequent conviction of from ten to 25 years – the same punishment, in other words, as a conviction for dealing in dagga.[84]

The Act included provisions for the deportation of non-South African citizens, if convicted, drastic forfeiture provisions of both movable and immovable property, and a controversial clause which provided for the arrest and detention of any person (of no stated minimum age) reasonably suspected of withholding information regarding dagga dealing or failing to report suspicion of dagga use or dealing. In theory this allowed a suspect to be kept in prison indefinitely and, as a result of objections from the Association of Law Societies, the provision was amended, empowering the Attorney General where necessary to stop the interrogation of the suspect and order his/her immediate release.[85]

The Act was especially oppressive when compared with contemporary perceptions of dagga in other countries and associated dagga legislation. In Canada in 1970, a Commission of Inquiry into the Non-Medical Use of Drugs recommended that dagga be classified as a restricted drug under the Drug and Foods Act, rather than as a prohibited drug under the Narcotics Control Act. It also advocated the release under certain conditions of young 'experimenters', in order to reduce the number of convictions and criminal records, while monitoring the situation through constant review and research.[86]

Also in 1970, in the United States, John Kaplan, Professor of Law at Stanford University and former consultant to the California legislature on drugs, concluded that the laws governing dagga offences were as outmoded as those of the Prohibition era, and that the costs of combatting the drug far outstripped the supposed benefits. Instead he recommended that, as with alcohol, cannabis use should be controlled through licensing, quality control, price and non-sale to minors.

In the United Kingdom, in 1968, the Advisory Committee on Drug Dependence, under the chairmanship of Sir Edward Wayne, released its Report on Cannabis, noting in its covering memorandum to the Home Secretary that, while:

> the adverse effects which the consumption of cannabis in even small amounts may produce in some people should not be dismissed as insignificant we think that the dangers of its use as commonly accepted in the past and the risk of progression to opiates have been overstated, and that the existing criminal sanctions intended to curb its use are unjustifiably severe.[87]

The Hallucinogens Sub-Committee, under Baroness Wootton of Abinger, recommended *inter alia* that, while restrictions on dagga's availability should be maintained, possession of small amounts of the drug should not be regarded as a serious crime punishable by imprisonment. Instead the Sub-Committee recommended that the maximum punishment for the sale or supply of the drug be a fine and/or imprisonment of no more than two years. It also recommended that the legislation governing dagga be separate from the legislation dealing with heroin and other opiates.[88]

At least some of these recommendations appear to have been acceptable to the establishment: three years later, when the British Parliament passed the Misuse of Drugs Act of 1971, the statute separated controlled drugs into three classes in order of harmfulness. Class A included opium, morphine, LSD and cocaine, Class B dagga, codeine and amphetamine, and Class C lesser stimulants, such as benzphetamine. In addition, no minimum sentence was prescribed.[89]

In Australia in mid-1971, the Senate Select Committee on Drug Trafficking and Drug Abuse Report concluded that dagga does not cause physical dependence.[90] Alcohol and tobacco, on the other hand – the most widely used and abused drugs – are described as causing physical dependence as well as being potentially extremely harmful.[91]

In November of the same year, just two weeks before South Africa's Drugs Act of 1971 came into effect, the World Health Organization released a report based on studies by experts in the United States, Canada, India, Nigeria, Brazil, Egypt, the Netherlands and the United Kingdom, which indicated 'an association' between dagga use and minor crime/anti-social behaviour, but could find no link between dagga use and major crime.[92]

The Dutch were way ahead of everyone else. Like many other nations they had to abide by the international drug agreements. But recognising the difficulties and costs of *prohibiting* dagga use, they opted instead to *contain* it. Following the findings of a Government Commission in 1972, illicit drugs were divided into two categories. One consisted of drugs deemed dangerous, including heroin and cocaine. The second, less dangerous, group included dagga. The law was altered, making possession of up to 30 grams of dagga a misdemeanour. The sale of dagga was permitted in licensed coffee shops.[93]

Compared to this worldwide softening of attitudes, those of South Africa's establishment were virtually fossilised. The introduction of the 1971 Drugs Act effectively shut down all debate regarding the pros and cons of licensing or liberalising the use of dagga. Writing just as it came into operation, Professor Ellison Kahn voiced his concern that '[i]f the threat of punishment held out by the new Act does not prove a very strong deterrent, one may wonder what is to happen to our already crowded gaols – looking at the matter from a practical and not a humanitarian standpoint'. He anticipated that it could so happen 'that where a minimum period of imprisonment has to be imposed courts will tend frequently to suspend all but an insubstantial part of sentences, at least with first offenders'.[94]

In the first convictions under the new legislation, three days after the Drugs Act came into effect, the Pietermaritzburg magistrate's court did just that, in a case where seven men had pleaded guilty to possession of dagga. The sentences ranged from six months' imprisonment down to 21 days', with three youths of 19, 17 and 16, receiving six, six and four strokes of the cane respectively.[95]

Certain amendments were made to the Act over the next few years. In 1978, for example, judicial discretion was restored with regard to offences involving dagga, and in 1986 the principle of mandatory minimum sentences was abandoned, the penalties for possession and dealing, though, being substantially increased.[96] Finally, in 1992, the 1971 Act was repealed by the Drugs and Drug Trafficking Act 140 of 1992.

So what has changed? Not much. As Hoctor *et al.* note, the 1992 Act 're-enacts almost unchanged the prohibitions upon dealing in and possession of drugs contained in the 1971 Act'. Offences involving dagga are still not treated as any less serious than those involving 'hard' drugs. Instead, dagga is designated an 'undesirable dependence-producing substance', for which the more severe penalties are prescribed.[97]

The Act sets no minimum quantity of the drug that must be involved to constitute an offence, and introduces the notion of 'vicarious liability' by principals for the acts of their employees or agents.[98] Imprisonment for dealing in dagga is mandatory, for a period of up to 25 years, or both imprisonment and a fine (although the period of imprisonment may be suspended in part or as a whole). In 1997, the Criminal Law Amendment Act 105 of 1997, reintroduced mandatory minimum sentences for certain offences. For example, unless there are substantial and compelling circumstances justifying a lesser sentence, a first conviction for dealing in dagga valued at more than R50 000 carries a sentence of not less than 15 years, a second not less than 20, and for a third or subsequent offence, not less than 25.[99]

Perhaps the only important change is that in 1996 the Constitutional Court ruled the *presumptions* to be unconstitutional, in that they offended against the usual presumption of innocence.[100]

It is no exaggeration then to say that in 2015 South Africa's drug laws remain virtually as draconian as they had been in 1971. And dagga remains the main target against which South African drug legislation is directed.

The South African legislature continues to regard dagga as a considerable social evil. As recently as 2000, the Supreme Court of Appeal held that the use of dagga, particularly in large doses, is harmful to both the individual user and society at large – a decision subsequently upheld by the Constitutional Court.[101]

The SCA also accepted the long-discredited bogey that dagga is a 'stepping-stone' to the use of harder, more dangerous drugs.[102] Many of the fears which gave birth to the notorious Drugs Act of 1971, in other words, still remain and, if the debate surrounding dagga has moved on at all, it has done so only with baby steps. With the advent of democracy in 1994 and the implementation of our new constitution, the most obvious change in sentencing has, perhaps, been the abolition of caning.

For 40 years the unbroken official line has been that punitive drug laws work – that harsh penalties lower levels of drug use. This has finally been debunked. In 2014 the United Kingdom government's first evidence-based study admitted that, in the words of Minister Norman Baker, who together with the Home Secretary signed off the document, 'increasing sentences does not stop drug use'.[103]

5

Chocolate, coffee & cannabis

*I have measured out my life
with coffee spoons.*

(T.S. Eliot: Gardner (ed.) 1973: 874)

The demonisation of dagga in South Africa appears even more oppressive – and illogical – when compared with legal mood-altering substances, such as caffeine and even chocolate.

Chocolate contains an interesting compound called anandamide, which has been shown to bind to the same receptor in the brain as tetrahydrocannabinol (THC), the active ingredient in dagga. Although the structure of anandamide is quite different from the structure of THC, the fact that both are mood-altering drugs which bind to the same receptors in the brain, raises a rather interesting issue. As chemists Couteur and Burreson put it: 'If anandamide is responsible

Anandamide from chocolate [left] and THC from marijuana [right] are structurally different.[104]

for the feel-good appeal that many people claim for chocolate, then we could ask a provocative question: What is it we want to outlaw, the THC molecule or its mood-altering effect? If it is the mood-altering effect, should we be considering making chocolate illegal?'[105]

If so, we should perhaps also consider making coffee illegal – since coffee contains not only anandamide but caffeine, another psychoactive drug.[106]

Caffeine was introduced into Europe in the early 1500s, through cocoa, or chocolate as the Aztecs' 'drink of the gods' came to be called. A century later, caffeine usage received a major boost with the arrival of a more concentrated form of the alkaloid in the form of coffee, and it is as coffee, arguably the world's most popular stimulant, that caffeine is most easily accessed today. In 2004 the world's population consumed the equivalent of 120 000 tonnes of pure caffeine per annum, just over half of it in the form of coffee.[107] Ten years on, that figure is likely to be substantially higher.

Some idea of the power of caffeine is illustrated by

Spiders on drugs: web (d) produced under the influence of caffeine shows the most serious damage.[108]

(a) a normal web, spun by a drug-free spider

b) web spun under the influence

(c) ... of benzadrine of dagga ...

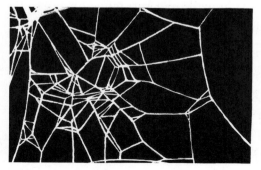

and (d) ... of caffeine

experiments conducted on the web-spinning abilities of the common house spider under the influence of various psychotropic drugs. The experiments were conducted by NASA, the United States' National Aeronautics and Space Administration, in the 1990s. The mind-altering substances under which the arachnids performed ranged from sleeping pills to LSD, and almost everything in-between, including caffeine and dagga. The results were startling. The drug which most seriously impaired the spider's web-spinning abilities was caffeine.[109]

Caffeine is not just mood and mind altering, it is also addictive. And dangerous. While no deaths have been recorded from overdosing on dagga,[110] it is possible to die from a caffeine overdose. About 10 grams – roughly 100 cups of coffee consumed in quick succession – will kill an adult. Less than three and a half grams can kill a child. Caffeine intoxication can also cause psychosis and produce hallucinations. American truck drivers have reported being chased by balls of white light while under its influence and some researchers have blamed caffeine intoxication for the widespread belief in Unidentified Flying Objects in the US.[111]

The earliest surviving record of coffee drinking is that of Rhazes, an Arab physician in the tenth century, but the Ethiopians are believed to have drunk coffee well before then. An ancient Ethiopian myth tells of how some goats belonging to a herder named Kaldi became 'frisky and started to dance around on their hind legs' after consuming the leaves and berries of a certain tree. Kaldi, upon eating the same bright red berries, found their effects to be as exhilarating as his goats did. He gave a sample to a local holy man, who disapprovingly threw them onto a fire. The aroma which arose from the flames was too delicious to ignore, and the roasted beans were quickly retrieved, resulting in the first recorded cup of coffee. Not everyone approved of coffee's power, and from time to time, coffee drinking was illegal. By the end of the fifteenth century, however, Muslim pilgrims had carried coffee to all parts of the Islamic world, and by the seventeenth century it had also spread to Europe. And spread it did – like wildfire. By 1700 there were over 2 000 coffee shops in London alone.

Ironically, coffee is credited with an increase in sobriety in Europe since to a certain extent it replaced the consumption of ale for breakfast in the north and wine in the south.[112] In certain segments of society, dagga may well perform the same function. As mentioned already, devotees of dagga are generally far less prone to violence when intoxicated than drinkers of alcohol. Perhaps dagga will one day be as legal as the once-outlawed coffee. It is already happening. Uruguay in South America has ended its prohibition of recreational dagga. In February 2015, on the birthday of Jamaican reggae legend Bob Marley, Jamaica passed a bill decriminalising the possession of small amounts of dagga for personal use.[113] The previous year, four states in the United States of America – Oregon, Washington, Colorado and Alaska – had also legalised the sale and possession of the drug for recreational use. Twenty-three other states have implemented some form of decriminalisation.

Central to the legislation are regulations protecting the young. In Washington state, for example, while specialised stores are allowed to sell dagga cookies, they are not permitted to put dagga into lollipops or other sweets which might appeal to children. Dagga products are prohibited from carrying any labelling or packaging designed to appeal to children, and all products containing dagga must by law be clearly labelled.[114]

The taxation, regulation and sale of dagga in a strictly conditional manner to tobacco and alcohol, has been heralded as a progressive step in a decades-long fight to legalise recreational dagga. Addressing a party to celebrate Oregon's new drug legislation, Congressman Earl Blumenauer noted that the movement to decriminalise dagga was gaining momentum: 'You are going to change national policy,' he told supporters. 'The marijuana legalization train has left the station.'[115]

6

A booming industry

Correction:
> *In the handicrafts exhibition at Wordsley*
> *Community Centre, the contribution of the*
> *Misses Smith was 'smocking and rugs', and*
> *not 'smoking and drugs' as stated in last*
> *week's report.*

(Stourbridge County Express: Hill 2011: 209)

Dagga has been around for thousands of years. It is deeply embedded in human history and culture. In traditional southern African society, dagga was the recreational drug of choice, and for centuries its use was regarded as legitimate and acceptable.[116] With its criminalisation, however, dagga went underground and its use today is not openly admitted.[117] Which is not really surprising, considering the draconian legislation the South African state amassed against it. But that doesn't mean people stopped using dagga. They just stopped using it openly.

Despite its illegality, dagga is a booming industry. The so-called southern African cannabis complex, consisting of South Africa, Lesotho and Swaziland, is believed to be one of the largest dagga-producing regions in the world. But because dagga is illegal, the dagga trade is not taxed, and does not benefit the State. At the same time, dagga's criminalisation, and the destructive activities of associated organised crime syndicates, places an increasing burden on those of us who do pay tax.

It gets worse. In February 2015, for example, the South African Police Service chemically 'bombed' the crops of villagers around Lusikisiki, in the old Transkei, whom they suspected of growing dagga. The chemicals, sprayed from helicopters over a wide area, included glyphosate. A highly toxic herbicide better known by its marketing name 'RoundUp', glyphosate can be extremely harmful to the environment, endangering the livestock that eat the remains of treated crops, reducing the fertility of the soil and polluting the rivers and springs. At Lusikisiki, it destroyed not only dagga plants, but also all the other crops, including gardens of mealies, beans and pumpkins.[118]

In three weeks over 500 hectares were poisoned. The Lusikisiki region is one of the most poverty-stricken areas in South Africa. The people here are among the poorest of our poor. They have next to nothing. And now they have even less. The victims included a widow with five children in her care, including three grandchildren, whose survival depends on her social care grant and what she can grow in her fields. The police justified their actions in the name of the war against drugs. The villagers see it differently. As a war on our own people. In one stroke, the local village economy had been eviscerated. Meanwhile, in Johannesburg, the sudden shortage of dagga has doubled the price; city gangsters aren't complaining.[119]

For subsistence farmers, such as the people of the Lusikisiki region, dagga is a means of supplementing their meagre incomes. Because it's illegal, they are not able to grow dagga as a large-scale cash crop. But if they could they would and, in the process, perhaps break free of the chains of poverty that have bound them and their families for generations.

Actual figures are difficult to establish, but the southern African cannabis complex is potentially enormously lucrative. In 1992, the South African government estimated that 6 000 hectares of land were under dagga cultivation, while the USA's Drug Enforcement Agency's estimate for the same period was 20 000 to 30 000 hectares. The very nature of the trade – its illegality and secrecy – also makes it difficult to estimate either the quantity of dagga produced in South Africa or its monetary value. Most of this dagga is traded internally, within southern Africa. The market is believed to be enormous, certainly a multi-billion-dollar industry, estimated as far back as 1994 as topping 180 000 tonnes annually in production, to

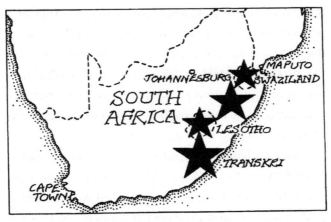

The Southern African cannabis complex.

the value of about US$15 billion.[120] Two decades on, these figures may well have doubled.

Today, most dagga cultivation is concentrated in three regions: South Africa's Pondoland in the former Transkei region, Lesotho's Mokhotlong district, and Swaziland's Hhohho district centred around Piggs Peak. Although the majority of southern African dagga producers grow only enough to supplement their income, at Hhohho alone 70 per cent of agricultural income is derived from dagga.[121] Were producers permitted to grow dagga without fear of prosecution, that figure would surely increase – and yield potentially enormous taxable profits.

Nor should the question of crime syndicates be ignored. Illegality favours increased criminality, just as the prohibition of alcohol in the United States in the 1930s favoured the rise of the Mafia. The further it travels from its source of origin, the greater the value of the drug, and the greater the profits. As things stand at the moment, drug gangs involved in trafficking dagga, and in all other kinds of related illegal activities, are pretty much the main, if not only, beneficiaries of the drug's criminalisation.

One disadvantage in the Netherland's liberal dagga policy[122] was that, although the 'cannabis cafés' were legal, their supply chain was not. Sourced from illicit dealers and smugglers, dagga remained unfree from smugglers and organised-crime syndicates.[123] The best way around this, as a recent opinion piece put it, and the best way to protect the people who use drugs such as dagga, 'is not to create a lucrative black market controlled by lethal gangsters. It is to do precisely the opposite: legalise and regulate the use of drugs'.[124] It is a sentiment echoed by Sir William Patey, Britain's former ambassador to Afghanistan, in a similar context:

> If we cannot deal effectively with [illegal] supply, then the only alternative would seem to me to try to limit the demand for illicit drugs by making a licit supply of them available from a legally regulated market.[125]

Should dagga be licensed and legalised, those same syndicates which currently profit from its covert

Cannabis starter kits for sale, Amsterdam, 2014 (photo courtesy Eric Leach).

distribution would be liable for substantial taxation. Other problems associated with illegality, including pushers and the financial incentives that drive the corruption of police and prison warders, would also be minimised or removed. Our prisons would be less overcrowded and our courts freed up to deal with the backlog of more serious crime. Perhaps the last word on dagga should go to Dr Franz Trautmann of the Trimbos Institute – the Netherlands institute for mental health and addiction – 'We are talking about a drug that is still problematic but by prohibition you make the problem bigger than it is'.[126]

Talking about dagga – or rather not talking about it – is part of the problem. It is such an emotionally charged subject, that a rational, national debate on the subject sometimes appears to be little more than a pipe-dream.

Here's just one recent example. In June 2014, online media carried a story headlined *Convicted woman seeks freedom to care for pregnant goat,* which claimed :'An Mpumalanga mother of three, convicted of possession of dagga, asked to be released from jail so she could attend to her neighbour's injured pregnant goat.'[127]

The real story was less sensational. The woman had pleaded guilty to the charge, explaining in mitigation that, although she knew it was illegal to sell dagga, as an unemployed widow she had hoped to use the profits to help support her three children. While awaiting sentencing, she had learnt that her seven-year-old child had 'beaten up' her neighbour's pregnant goat, and asked the court to temporarily release her in order to attend, not to the goat, but to her wayward child. (The court refused).

Internet chat rooms mushroomed, the comments ranging from tolerant to medieval, from *Don't judge her you are not God* to *She's still stoned*, with a whole gambit of advice in-between, ranging from *beat the kid* to *eat the goat.* One confused individual believed the goat had beaten up the child. Another scaled new heights with *ELEPHANT BULLCRAP.* As the clamour rose, the intellectual level fell; apart from the odd *I agree* or *Yebo*, it seems everyone was so busy talking, no one was listening.

Unfortunately the same sort of frenzied emotionality has characterised the dagga debate on more formal platforms. For a drug that induces a sense of mellowness in its users, dagga seems to have an extraordinary ability to provoke hysteria among its detractors.

7

Medicinal highs & lows: The current debate

They used to tell me, 'Drugs can kill you.'
Now that I'm 58, they are saying, 'Drugs
can save your life.' I realize my doctor is my
dealer now. He's a lot harder to get hold of.

(Robin Williams:[128] Jarski 2010: 489)

Dagga is one of the world's oldest cultivated crops. It is never going to be stamped out, regardless of how many laws are made. Dagga has played an integral part in many different cultures in many different ways through many centuries. From the San of southern Africa to the ancient Indians, dagga has also played a mystical, even religious role.[129]

Its most visible modern disciples are probably the Rastafarians, of whom the largest community by far is found in Jamaica, where two-thirds of the population use dagga for its religious, medicinal and healing properties. For men, women and children of all ages, smoking dagga is an essential part of religious worship. The Rastas consider dagga a sacred herb, a gift from Jah (God) to aid meditation, citing the Book of Psalms, 104: 14, which states: 'He causeth the grass for the cattle, and herb for the service of man'.

Cannabis sativa is believed to have been introduced to Jamaica in about 1845, brought to the island by indentured East Indian servants, as a result of which it is most commonly known there by a Hindi word *ganja*.[130] For most Rastafarians outside Jamaica, including those in South Africa, the sacred herb's preferred name remains *ganja*. Jamaica's recent decriminalisation of dagga for personal use has effectively legitimised the religious practices of a large percentage of its population. For South African Rastafarians there is still a long way to go.

In 2000, having completed his law degree, a young South African Rastafarian by the name of Garreth Prince applied to be admitted as an attorney. His application was refused on the grounds that he had two previous convictions for possession of dagga and that as a Rastafarian he had expressed his intention to continue to possess the drug in future. On the basis that the Drugs Act 140 of 1992, and Medicines Act 101 of 1965, infringed the appellant, Prince's rights to freedom of religion, the case went to the High Court, then to the Supreme Court of Appeal and all the way up to the Constitutional Court, which found against him. The Court determined that, in a democratic society, the Legislature had the power and duty to ensure the prohibition of conduct which it considered to be anti-social, and to enforce that prohibition by criminal sanctions. The granting of permission for Rastafarians to possess dagga would undermine that prohibition and further, that the appellant had not applied for an exemption solely for religious purposes, nor on behalf of the Rastafarian Houses.[131]

There is evidence to suggest that the ancient Israelites too used dagga to commune with God (see Appendix 1). But in the face of alternative religions, the modern western religious establishment tends to be defensive. The current head of the Catholic Church, Pope Francis, for example, who is regarded as being perhaps the most liberal Pope to date, recently spoke out against the legalisation of recreational drugs. 'The problem of drug use is not solved with drugs,' he intoned. And with that, as one newspaper put it, 'prospects of a liberal Vatican view on dagga went up in smoke'.[132]

Dagga has also long been used medicinally. Contrary to claims made in South Africa's so-called 'Drugs Act' 41 of 1971 and its supporters, that dagga has 'no medicinal value', and 'no practical medicinal uses',[133] its medicinal properties have been recognised for hundreds of years. The *Venidad*, an ancient Persian religious text dating back to the seventh century BC, lists dagga as the most important of 10 000 medicinal plants.[134] Dagga's medicinal properties are also mentioned in *De Materia Medica*. Written in about 70 AD by Pedanius Dioscorides, a Greek physician who travelled widely throughout the Roman Empire as an army doctor, collecting and studying medicinal plants, *De Materia Medica* became the most important medical text for the next 1 500 years.[135]

Chinese medical practitioners, the most advanced in the ancient world, also recognised dagga's medicinal properties. By the second century AD, Chinese physicians were able to perform major invasive surgery with the aid of an anaesthetic called *ma-fei-san*, a mixture of dagga and aconite, a plant belonging to the buttercup family. As early as the fourth century AD dagga was used in Palestine, which included present-day Israel, to ease the pain of childbirth. By the eighth century, it was well incorporated into Arabic medical knowledge systems. In India its medicinal properties were mentioned in the *Anandakanda*, thought to have been written in about the tenth century AD. Its uses included the treatment of cholera and delirium tremens, the relief of rheumatism and pain, and the promotion of 'great mental cheerfulness'. It was also used as an aphrodisiac and appetite stimulant, and as an anti-vomiting agent.[136]

By the second half of the eighteenth century dagga was included in dispensatories (medical textbooks consulted by pharmacists and physicians) throughout Europe. Dagga was most often recommended as an antibiotic and pain-killer[137] – pretty much the same uses it had had in ancient Palestine, India and here in South Africa.

As mentioned in a previous chapter, prior to dagga's criminalisation in South Africa it was widely used in Afrikaner home-remedies, for the treatment of ailments ranging from high blood pressure to bleeding and snake bite. The Afrikaners learnt much of their bush-craft from the indigenous peoples, and dagga has an even longer history of usage amongst traditional doctors and *izisangoma*, who used it to treat a great variety of ailments, including blood poisoning, anthrax, dysentery, snake bite, malaria and blackwater fever.[138] Today, as Tony Dold, Curator of the Selmar Schonland Herbarium at Rhodes University, points out, although dagga is 'not openly traded', throughout South Africa it continues to be 'used medicinally by lots of people, mostly for asthma and chest problems but also for *amafufunyana* – mental illness'.[139]

Dagga also has veterinary properties – in earlier times it was used in the treatment of African horse sickness. People in the Karoo sometimes fed a little dagga to their horses, 'to give them some extra get-up-and-go': 'They seemed to love it,' says resident Peet van Heerden. 'On a Saturday morning, mounted labourers would often stop over at a farm near Murraysburg. There they would get an ear of dagga and feed it to their horses, who would then merrily canter into town well before the bottle store closed.'[140]

Rich in amino acids and unsaturated fats, minerals, vitamins and protein, dagga seeds are a useful foodstuff for birds in the wild, rabbits and other small animals. Dagga also acts as a mental tonic. The brains of every animal species utilised in dagga research have been found to have the same cannabinoid receptors as the human brain and, in recent studies, dagga-using animal models behaved in much the same way as dagga-using humans. They got stoned. Or, as one scientist put it, did a lot of 'non-targeted staring into space'.[141]

Relaxation and euphoria, often accompanied by mirth, are dagga's most characteristic effects, so it is not surprising that one of its first medical uses in the west was as an anti-depressant. As early as 1621, Robert Burton, a cleric at St Thomas the Martyr, Oxford, championed dagga as an anti-depressant in his *Anatomy of Melancholy*.[142] It was also used in treating depression in the early twentieth century, but discontinued in the 1950s with the development of anti-depressant drugs.[143]

Studies in the United States in the late 1970s have shown that dagga can also help prevent blindness in patients suffering from glaucoma, by decreasing the pressure inside the eye. More recent studies in the States have shown that tetrahydrocannabinol can help treat loss of appetite and slow down weight-loss in cancer patients, and in those suffering from AIDS and other illnesses. The Food and Drug Administration has approved two synthetic cannabinoids – dronabinol and nabilone – for the treatment of nausea and vomiting in cancer patients undergoing chemotherapy, where other standard drugs have failed. Dagga's anti-inflammatory, pain-relieving properties have proved to be several hundred times more effective than aspirin, and a 2006 study by the prestigious Scripps Research Institute has shown that, by blocking an enzyme which causes the progression of Alzheimer's, dagga can slow the advance of the disease.[144]

Can South Africa learn anything from this? We have one of the most progressive and enlightened constitutions in the world, yet our drug legislation lags far behind. Of especial concern is the question of whether or not dagga 'deserves' to be subject to such drastic legislation[145] (see Appendix 2).

Moves to legalise dagga for medical use are gradually gaining ground, albeit very slowly and spasmodically. As Dr Umberto Veronesi, a leading cancer physician and former Italian Health Minister noted when Italy legalised medicinal dagga in 2013, dagga 'is a very effective medicine, but since it's also a drug ... there's always fear'.[146]

Reservations about legalising or even licensing dagga still revolve around the same issues which have always plagued it: fears of 'escalation' to harder drugs, impaired respiratory function, cardiovascular complications, the potentially adverse impact on the development of teenagers, and general anti-social behaviour. Nevertheless, at a community level the harms associated with dagga are a lot lower than those associated with alcohol and tobacco use,[147] and the financial and medicinal advantages of decriminalisation cannot be compared.

It is this, dagga's medicinal properties, and especially its efficacy in reducing pain in cancer patients, which has recently brought it to the fore again in South Africa. In 2014, Professor Charles Parry, Director of the Alcohol, Tobacco and Other Drug Research Unit at the Medical Research Council, called upon the government to allow human trials on medicinal dagga use, especially to assist people with HIV/Aids. Although medical use of dagga is now legal in Austria, Canada, Finland, Germany, Italy, Israel, the Netherlands, Portugal and Spain, as well as some parts of the United States, said Parry, in South Africa research into the safety of legalising dagga for medicinal use has been severely hampered by a lack of human trials. 'The South African government,' wrote Parry, 'should make it easier for researchers to conduct studies ... and funding should be made available to support this research.'[148]

In February of that same year, 2014, Dr Mario Oriani-Ambrosini, an opposition Member of Parliament suffering from stage four cancer, urged the government to consider making dagga legal in South Africa for medical purposes in a regulated research-controlled environment. Decriminalising dagga for medicinal use, he argued, would help millions of

South Africans suffering from his condition, as well as contributing to the transformation of the country's health sector.[149]

Oriani-Ambrosini's plea, serendipitously following a similar proposal by Lord Maurice Saatchi in the United Kingdom's House of Lords, received a standing ovation from Parliament and unprecedented support from the public. To the surprise of many, the current South African government publicly stated its willingness to re-open debate on the subject.[150]

Mario Oriani-Ambrosini, however, did not live to win his battle for the legalisation of medicinal dagga. In the terminal stages of lung cancer, he committed suicide at his home in Hout Bay on 16 August 2014. In an interview shortly before his death he said: 'Marijuana really has a positive effect – all the studies have shown this. It's an absolute crime not to allow it. It's nothing short of a human rights violation'.[151] Just one month later his Medical Innovation Bill (MIB) ran into its first hurdle, with the opposition Democratic Alliance refusing to support its proposals to legalise and regulate the use of cannabinoids.[152]

It took almost nine months for the MIB to come before the Parliamentary Portfolio Committee on Health. Briefing the Committee on 27 May 2015, Professor Charles Parry of the Medical Research Council (MRC) commended the late Ambrosini and acknowledged 'increasing evidence' of the value of cannabinoids in palliative care. However, he said the

MRC did not support the Bill in its current form. This was largely due to concerns over the Bill's promotion not only of medicinal dagga but of legalisation in general. Further clinical trials regarding the use of medicinal dagga were also needed.[153] The Medical Research Council emphasised that, as a public health research organisation, it did not support the smoking of dagga, just as it did not support the smoking of tobacco.[154]

Apart from humanitarian considerations, there are also substantial financial gains to be made from the medicinal dagga market. Recent reports note that Canada, for example, has been able to create 'a fast-growing, profitable and federally regulated industry with a distinct appeal to the more daring global investor'. In June 2014, Reuters reported that:

> About a dozen producers of the drug will find themselves in the spotlight this year as they consider going public or preparing to do so through share sales or reverse takeovers to capitalize on recent regulatory changes, investment bankers say.
>
> The companies are in a race to raise money to build facilities, attract patients and grab shares in a market projected to grow to $1.3-billion (R12.8-billion) in the next 10 years.
>
> The gateway has been opened by medicinal marijuana being made legal nationwide.[155]

It is still too early to predict what will happen in South Africa, but as our nation's medicinal needs grow, so too does our prison population, many of whom would not be there but for our draconian dagga laws.

By 2014, the cost of arresting and convicting a *single* low-level dagga user had ballooned to R240 000 – money which, as activists point out, would be far better spent fighting high-priority crimes.[156] The demands on our overstrained legal system and overburdened taxpayers grow apace. Dagga is a multi-billion buck business. According to one recent estimate, annual global dagga sales are worth US$150 billion to US$200 billion – at the current exchange rate, that's R1 500 billion to R2 000 billion per year.[157] With our booming population and shrinking tax base it would be criminal not to tax our slice of the pie.

Whatever debates continue to rage around the issues of licensing, legalisation and taxation of dagga, its medicinal and economic benefits or otherwise, the petty criminality of its adherents and mafia-style distribution syndicates, and so on, one thing about dagga which cannot be denied is its tendency to relax its adherents.

For those smokers who are too 'relaxed' to even hold their own pipes, here's one which requires no effort at all, but can be stuck in the ground and smoked while reclining:

A Zimbabwean hands-free dagga pipe.[158]

APPENDIX 1

God on high

When Linnaeus named *Cannabis sativa* in 1753, he based the first word on *kannabis*, the classical Greek word for hemp, derived from the Sanskrit *cana*. *Cana* means 'cane' while *bis* is believed to come from the Hebrew *bosm* or Aramaic *busma*, meaning 'aromatic'. Dagga's full generic name, *Cannabis sativa*, then, may be translated as 'cultivated fragrant cane'.[159]

The possibility of a Hebrew link is interesting because the ancient Israelites are known to have been in constant contact with dagga-using cultures. A more direct link, however, was drawn in 1936 by an etymologist named Sula Benet of the Institute of Anthropological Sciences in Warsaw, who claimed to have found Biblical references to the use of dagga, as both an incense and as a psychoactive drug.[160]

Benet's evidence came from Exodus 30, verses 22–33, in which God instructs Moses to produce a holy anointing oil, one of the ingredients of which is *kaneh bosm*. Previously, scholars had presumed this to have meant *calamus*, a fragrant water plant. Their claim, however, appears to have been based on erroneous Greek translations of the Old Testament, and does not 'fit' with the effects of the said anointing oil. As Old Testament texts show, the oil was used by the ancient Hebrews to put themselves into a trance, during which God 'spoke' to them.

The trance and everything associated with the ritual was 'other-worldly'. The oil was accorded such great importance that it was a criminal offence to compound it for anything but a holy purpose. The act of anointing was associated 'with the outpouring of the Spirit of God', and conducted with solemnity. The word 'anointed' was associated with the bestowal of divine favour and, though accepted without question, the anointed was sometimes described as a 'madman'[161] – all of which suggests the euphoria or 'high' associated with dagga. And, of course, there's the undeniable linguistic similarity of *kaneh bosm* to *kannabis*.

Subsequent research has supported Benet's hypothesis. Recent scholarship has suggested that dagga was widely used in Hebrew temples up until 621 BC, when it was suppressed during the reign of the reformer king, Josiah. Some scholars, however, believe that its medicinal usage continued long afterwards, and that Christ may have administered dagga-based oils in his healing, including his treatment of eye or skin ailments.[162] And while the use of oil in anointing the sick may be understood as an invocation of the Holy Spirit,[163] it could just as easily speak to dagga's well-known medicinal properties.

APPENDIX 2

Mistaken identity?

As in South Africa, dagga was once legal in Britain.

In British India, the drug had been prevalent, enjoyed by members of all castes from the Brahmins to the Banias, as a medicine, a recreational drug, and in their religious ceremonies. In Britain itself, however, dagga had maintained a rather low profile until about the middle of the nineteenth century. Although a number of Englishmen in India had written about it, it was left to an Irish-born doctor, William Brooke O'Shaughnessy, to write the first definitive account of dagga and almost single-handedly popularise its usage in Britain.

Having graduated as a medical doctor at just twenty-one, O'Shaughnessy had headed off to India, where he was soon engaged in a number of experiments with local medicinal drugs on both people and animals, with dagga rapidly taking centre stage. The results of his observations and experiments were published in several journals, culminating in 1842 in his *Bengal*

Dispensatory and Companion to the Pharmacopoeia, in which the section on dagga ran to 25 pages.[164]

O'Shaughnessy, incidentally, also invented the saline drip, and was a pioneer of the 'electric telegraph'. He went on to become Director General of Telegraphs in India, supervising the building of India's first telegraphic network, which is widely believed to have 'saved the Indian Empire for Britian' during the so-called Indian Mutiny, and for which he was knighted in 1856.[165] But it was his work on dagga that first caught the public's attention.

O'Shaughnessy's *Bengal Dispensatory* was the first and most comprehensive assessment of dagga's medicinal and narcotic properties to be published and the first based on first-hand studies, by no less an authority than a Doctor of Medicine, Professor of Chemistry and Honorary Fellow of the Royal Medico-Botanical Society of London. His conclusion: that dagga was 'a wonder-drug'.[166]

British doctors responded with enthusiasm, as shown in the *Provincial Medical and Surgical Journal* of 1842. But the drug really took off a year later. On a visit to London in 1843, O'Shaughnessy persuaded a pharmacist named Peter Squire to produce a medicinal tincture for his personal use from some hashish he'd brought back with him from India. Squire's efforts produced the first recorded extract of dagga in alcohol, which he patented as Squire's Extract and marketed as an analgesic. Taken up by other pharmacists, it was made under license in the United States as Tilden's Extract. Both medicines were widely used and highly valued for their pain-killing properties. In 1850 dagga was included in the *United States Pharmacopoeia* as a treatment for, among other things, neuralgia, dysentery, alcoholism and opiate addiction, uterine haemorrhaging and convulsions.[167]

In the latter part of the nineteenth century, doctors often prescribed dagga-based analgesic medicines in preference to opium, since the latter was highly addictive, while dagga was not. This was especially so after the American Civil War, which saw a rapid rise in the use of morphine, a highly addictive opium derivative, by ex-servicemen as well as widows trying to cope with their grief. Dagga was also preferred in so far as it did not produce any of the other negative side effects of opium use, such as loss of appetite, excessive itching and chronic constipation. In fact, other than euphoria and drowsiness, dagga in moderate doses appeared to have no adverse side effects at all.[168]

Some scholars have linked dagga's subsequent decline to the advent of synthetic drugs, made possible by the huge advances in chemistry in the late nineteenth century. But dagga was also perhaps a victim of mistaken identity. And with that, 'a great medicinal opportunity [was] missed'.[169]

As the twentieth century loomed and more was understood about the destructive and addictive properties of opiates, calls for their prohibition increased internationally.[170] And dagga somehow got caught up in the groundswell.

The first International Opium Commission was held in 1909 – in Shanghai of all places, once the centre of the world's opium trade. A second convention was held two years later at The Hague, in the Netherlands. Only a dozen countries were represented, yet they took it upon themselves to construct an international framework for drug legislation. The South African delegation proposed that dagga be treated as being as addictive as opiates, and the conference agreed to look into the matter. The First World War put a temporary stop to further discussions but, with its end, brought another wave of opiate addicts into the public eye. Three years after the end of the war-to-end-all-wars the League of Nations established an Advisory Committee on Traffic in Opium and Other Dangerous Drugs. The fact that prominent member countries, most notably the British, had made a mint of money out of drugs, including taxing dagga in India and peddling opium to China,[171] was apparently not an issue. And another war, which continues to this day, began.

In 1922, the South African government passed the Customs and Excise Duties Amendment Act 35 of 1922, prohibiting the importation, conveyance, sale and supply, use and possession of habit-forming drugs, including dagga. The cultivation of dagga, at this stage, was not outlawed. But a year later, in November 1923, the Secretary to the South African Prime Minister wrote to the League of Nations Advisory Committee on Traffic in Opium, complaining that dagga was still not included on the International List of Habit-forming Drugs, and strongly suggesting that the various governments party to the International Opium Convention be asked to do so.[172]

This was followed in 1924 and 1925 by two opium conventions at which, although concerned with habit-forming opiates, the non-habit-forming, non-opiate dagga found itself firmly on the agenda. The second of these, the 1925 International Convention on Narcotic Control held in Geneva, prohibited the non-medical use of opiates internationally. At the behest of the Egyptian delegate, Mohammed El Guindy, with the Turks in accord, dagga was included in the prohibition. El Guindy's passionate plea included a startling statistic from the aptly named Egyptian Lunacy Department (run by an Englishman who could not speak Arabic) that the 'illicit use of hashish is the principle cause of most of the cases of insanity occurring in Egypt'. The majority of the delegates who, as one historian notes, 'knew nothing about cannabis, and who were there to argue about opium', did not object.[173]

In compliance with the resolutions taken at the 1925 Geneva Convention, in September 1928 – the same year in which South Africa promulgated the Medical, Dental and Pharmacy Act 13 of 1928, effectively outlawing everything to do with dagga, including its cultivation – dagga was added to the schedule of the

British Dangerous Drugs Act.[174]

Historians struggle to define the exact moment when dagga began its fall from grace on the international stage, and even more so its listing as an opiate. Certain moments stand out, but they don't really explain the *why* behind the *what*. In 1916, for example, at the height of the First World War, rumours began to circulate about the use of opium and cocaine among off-duty soldiers in London. The authorities acted quickly: to keep them focused on fighting, they issued an order in the name of the Army Council prohibiting the sale of certain drugs to members of the Armed Forces. The order was aimed at opiates, including heroin, morphine and opium, but somehow dagga also made it on to the list. El Guindy's 'spectacular performance' at Geneva in 1925 is as perplexing an affair, and one which remains subject to much debate.[175]

The story of the demonisation of dagga is – to borrow a phrase from a slightly different context – 'one of shaky science, misjudgements and misunderstandings, media scares, and once-important but now long-dead political agendas'.[176]

Politicians are not known for their honesty, nor their lack of hypocrisy. And drugs seem to bring out the worst of both. Everyone knows about how Bill Clinton smoked dagga at university but claims not to have inhaled – but Newt Gingrich probably takes the cake.

In 1997, Speaker of the House Gingrich introduced into the United States Congress the Drug Importer Death Penalty Act. The Act held that anyone found guilty of importing what the US Attorney General considered a hundred doses of a controlled substance be sentenced to life imprisonment without the option of parole. Moreover, if the guilty party already had a previous conviction for a similar offence, the death penalty could be imposed.

The Act was passed in 2001. When Gingrich was reminded by journalists that years earlier he too had admitted smoking dagga at university, he Nkandla'd:

> When I smoked pot, it was illegal, but not immoral. Now it is illegal and immoral. The law didn't change, only the morality. That's why you get to go to jail and I don't.[177]

Quite how or why dagga had suddenly become 'immoral', he would or could not say. One is reminded of the words of the nineteenth-century clergyman, Sydney Smith: 'Whenever I enter a village, straightway I find an ass.'[178]

Endnotes

1 Van Riebeeck II: 286 & III: 259.
2 Dapper 1668: 41; Ten Rhyne 1686: 153; Crampton *et al.* 2013: 67; Thompson 1827 I: 52.
3 CA ACC 612 (34): 16 August 1886.
4 Kolbe 1731, vol. 1: 263. Hottentot is an offensive term for the Khoikhoi dating back to the seventeenth century. 'Khoikhoi' is itself not without controversy as it originally meant 'angry men', and was used by their San, or Bushman, adversaries. My thanks to Tony Dold for drawing my attention to this illustration, and for reading and commenting on this work; any remaining errors are mine.
5 See, for example, Mossop 1947: 136 fn 19; Kirby, editor of Smith *1834–6* I: 312 fn 1 & II: 254 fn 502 & Smith 1966: 196; Thom, editor of Van Riebeeck II: 286 fn 1.
6 W.A. Emboden, in Du Toit 1996: 128. For the chemical effects of dagga on the brain, see Castle & Murray 2004: 19–34.
7 Kolbe 1731, vol 1: 210; see also Ten Rhyne 1686: 153; Dapper 1668: 41, 47; Crampton *et al.*, 2013: 67.
8 Bensusan 1972: 116
9 *Boom* ('*tree*') is slang for dagga.
10 Burchell I: 366. Although 'San' is the preferred modern term for the Bushmen, it was originally a derogatory Khoikhoen word meaning 'rascal' or 'robber', and recently 'Bushman' has regained some of its popularity.
11 Burchell I: 379, 391, 416; Valentyn II: 5; Crampton, *et al.* 2013: 67, 163; Mentzel III: 85; Thompson I: 52. *Boer* literally means 'farmer' in Dutch. During the struggle against apartheid in the twentieth century *boer* was used to denote white agents of the racist regime, but here is used in its original meaning.
12 Kahn 1972: 114; Rosenthal 1973: 141.
13 Laidler 1928: 441.

14 Kahn 1972: 109, 114, 115; Hoctor *et al.*: F3-8.

15 Van Riebeeck II: 286 fn 1 & III: 257.

16 Bensusan 1972: 116.

17 Du Toit 1996: 127.

18 Smith 1834–6 I: 313. Symptoms of overdosing on THC or tetrahydrocannabinol, the psychotropic principle of dagga, include intense agitation, hallucinations and incoherence (Castle & Murray 2004: 1). For more on THC see chapter 3.

19 Abraham 1959 *NADA*: 70.

20 Booth 2003: 24.

21 Booth 1979: 25.

22 Du Toit 1996: 127, 128, 129.

23 Detail of Wentzel's 'Zuid-kust van Afrika' 1752, from Godée-Molsbergen 1922, III, facing page 264.

24 Van Riebeeck III: 303.

25 In at least one instance a secret compartment was especially built into a trailer, in which huge quantities of dagga could be concealed – 1433 kilograms, in the case of *S v Morehudi* 1999(2) SACR 664(SCA).

26 Annotated detail of Wentzel's 1752 'Zuid-kust van Afrika' in Molsbergen 1922. See MA 2130: Museum Africa, Johannesburg for Wentzel full colour, full size, certified copy of 1752.

27 Crampton 2014: 182

28 Wikar, in Crampton 2014: 181.

29 Gordon I fn 83; Du Toit 1980, quoted in Saugestad: 327; Smith *1834–6* I: 312; Caton-Thompson: 91. A Portuguese priest, João dos Santos, describes the cultivation of dagga in southern Mozambique and the Zambezi valley in the late 1500s: 'a certain herb ... exactly like an ear of coriander, resembling it greatly in the grain and ear, but not in the leaf, which is like that of a clove gilliflower' which is grown throughout the land and is called *bangue*. The locals dry the leaves and stalks, pound them to powder, and eat and drink them by the handful, 'after which they are quite satisfied and their stomachs are comforted'. They 'sustain themselves with this bangue for many days, and eat nothing else; and many of them assemble together to eat it, becoming as drunk as if they had taken a quantity of wine. All ... are very fond of this herb, and commonly use it, going about half drunk from its effects; and those who are accustomed to it do not take any pombe [millet beer], but are satisfied with bangue alone' (Dos Santos 1609 *RSEA* VII: 210).

30 Manson 2007: 36; Voigt 1983: 79.

31 Du Toit 1996: 127, 129, 130; Krige & Krige 1956: 215; Hammond-Tooke 1974: 59.

32 Kahn 1972:113.

33 See Kahn 1972: 113; Burchell II: 85; Smith 1966: 196;

Hammond-Tooke 1974: 112.

34 Somerville: 127; Webb & Wright V: 87; Bain 1826: 41–2; Crampton *et al.* 2013: 55; Williams 1983: 162.

35 See Booth 2003: 2.

36 Detail, from White 1800: 35.

37 For more see Junod I: 311; Lt. Boteler, in Owen 1823: 115.

38 Up to a litre of smoke may be inhaled in a single smoking session. With no filtration, hookahs 'are particularly harmful – causing all the same diseases as cigarettes, only more so' (Professor Guy Richards, University of the Witwatersrand, quoted in 'Hookahs are worse for you than cigarettes', Zinhle Mapumulo, *City Press*, 17 May 2015).

39 Junod I: 31, 312.

40 From Junod I: 344.

41 Junod I: 312–3.

42 Booth 2003: 1, 3, 9, 18, 21; Le Couteur & Burreson 2004: 130.

43 Paterson 2009: 15.

44 Booth 2003: 9.

45 From Le Couteur & Burreson 2004: 130.

46 Booth 2003: 2, 3, 7, 8; Le Couteur & Burreson 2004: 130; Bensusan 1972: 116; Paterson 2009: 17, 24. For more on cannabinoid chemistry, see Castle & Murray 2004: 3–13.

47 Bensusan 1972: 116; Dapper 1668: 41; Ten Rhyne 1686: 153. Grevenbroek (1695: 263) concurs: they make 'the plant Daggha ... into little cakes not exceeding in size the silver coin known in the vernacular as a rix dollar; and these they chew, as the Indians do opium and the Egyptians oetum. It puts them to sleep, but never maddens them.' For smoking dagga, see Valentyn c. 1702 (II: 5) & Mentzel c. 1732 (I: 85).

48 Booth 2003: 10.

49 Solowij 1999: 28; Castle & Murray 2004: 30, 41; Bensusan 1972: 118–9.

50 See Crampton 2014: 87; Paterson 2009: 14.

51 Paterson 2009: 38, 39.

52 Bensusan 1972: 121; www.news24.com, accessed 20 June 2014; Kahn 1972: 113. A 2010 study in the UK into the overall individual and social harmfulness of 20 different substances, rated alcohol the most damaging (Parry & Myers 2011: 706).

53 Paterson 2009: 43, 50.

54 Bouhill, 1912, quoted in Paterson 2009: 51.

55 Paterson 2009: 39.

56 Bensusan 1972: 116, 117.

57 Booth 2003: 14, 121, 195, 204–5.

58 Bensusan 1972: 118.

59 Paterson 2009: 55–7.

60 Paterson 2009: 2; Bensusan 1972: 117; Castle & Murray 2004:

xiii; 'Harmless, harmful or medicinal?', *Mail & Guardian*,
Johannesburg, 4 July 2014.

61 Castle & Murray 2004: xv.

62 Castle & Murray 2004: 30.

63 Solowij 1999: 36; Castle & Murray 2004: 48, 49.

64 None of the symptoms are permanent and cease with abstinence
(Booth 2003: 15)

65 Booth 2003: 16

66 The reasons are unknown but Cannabis grown in hot climates
produces a higher percentage of THC and less CBD than that
grown in cooler climates Booth 2003: 7), which is unfortunate
since CBD has also been shown to reduce or block convulsions,
as well as blocking the progression of animal models of human
rheumatoid arthritis (Castle & Murray 2004: 5, 6).

67 See Axelson 1998: 25; Raven-Hart 1967: 4.

68 See Dapper 1668: 41, 47; Grevenbroek 1695: 263.

69 Castle & Murray 2004: 46.

70 From Klatzow 2014: 147. Permission to reproduce courtesy of
Dr Klatzow & Zebra Press. Pers. Comm. 28 & 29 May 2015

71 'Harmless, harmful or medicinal?', *Mail & Guardian*, 4 July
2014; 'Where there's smoke ...', *Mail & Guardian*, 29 August,
2014; Booth 2003: 16.

72 Paterson 2009: 2. Cigarette smokers, too, are at risk, as they are
two to four times more likely to develop coronary disease than
non-smokers ('Where there's smoke ...', *Mail & Guardian*, 29
August 2014).

73 Hoctor. *et al.*: F3-8; 'Easy Writers', *Sunday Times*,
Johannesburg, 20 February 2011; Le Couteur & Burreson 2004:
251.

74 Booth 2003: 114.

75 'Did the Bard do dagga?', *Daily Dispatch*, 20 June 2011.

76 Booth 2003: 80.

77 Kahn 1972: 105. My thanks to Jeremy Pickering and Clive
Plasket for their reading of and comments on this chapter; any
remaining mistakes are mine.

78 Kahn 1972: 105.

79 Dr Stoffel van der Merwe, *Cape Times*, 5 February 1990, from
Maclennan: 55.

80 Quoted in Kahn 1972: 114.

81 Kahn 1972: 106.

82 Kahn 1972: 106, 108.

83 Hoctor *et al.*: F3-8.

84 Kahn 1972: 106–107.

85 Kahn 1972: 107, 109–111.

86 Kahn 1972: 112.

87 Cited in Kahn 1972: 111.

88 Kahn 1972: 111, 112.
89 Kahn 1972: 112.
90 Kahn 1972: 112; see also Castle & Murray 2004: 32.
91 Alcohol lowers inhibitions, impairs fine motor control and coordination, and reduces reaction time. In low concentrations, it is a mild central nervous depressant, producing mild euphoria, but high concentrations of alcohol in the bloodstream can result in coma and death (Klatzow 2014:133). While alcohol can significantly reduce one's ability to drive a vehicle or operate machinery safely, dagga causes relatively small impairment of driving skills (Solowij 1999: 35); users tend to drive more cautiously when under its influence (Castle & Murray 2004: 47).
92 Kahn 1972: 113.
93 Booth 2003: 338.
94 Kahn 1972: 115.
95 Kahn 1972: 115.
96 Hoctor *et al.*: F3-9.
97 Hoctor *et al.*: F3-5, F3-10.
98 Hoctor *et al.*: F3-6, F3-8.
99 Section 51(2) (a) of Act 105 of 1997; Hoctor *et al.*: F3-35.
100 Hoctor *et al.*: F3-32; *S v Bhulwana, S v Gwadiso* 1996(1) SA 388 (CC).
101 *Prince v President, Cape Law Society, and Others* 2002(2) SA 794 (CC).
102 See *Prince v President, Cape Law Society, and Others* 2000(3) SA 845 (SCA).
103 *Legalbrief Today*, 31 October 2014. Conversely, international experience from countries which have liberalised their dagga legislation suggests that decriminalisation and depenalisation do not increase use (Parry 2002: 696).
104 Le Couteur & Burreson 2004: 265.
105 Le Couteur & Burreson 2004: 264–5.
106 Wild 2004: 11.
107 Wild 2004: 11.
108 The results of the NASA study conducted in 1996 are freely available on any number of websites, including www.kscience.co.uk; www.beforeitsnews.com; and www.delightfulknowledge.com, to name just a few.
109 See Wild 2004: facing page 149.
110 It has been estimated that it would take around 800 joints to kill a dagga smoker, and even then the death would be due to carbon monoxide rather than cannabinoid poisoning. By comparison, tobacco and alcohol are far more dangerous – by some estimates, 300 ml of vodka or 60 mg of nicotine could be lethal (Booth 2003: 15) yet, like caffeine, are legal while dagga is not.

111 Wild 2004: 11–12.
112 Le Couteur & Burreson 2004: 265–6.
113 *Legalbrief,* 11 February 2015.
114 *Weekend Post*, 19 July 2014.
115 *Mail & Guardian*, 30 May 2014, 7 November 2014 & 21 November 2014.
116 Hoctor *et al.*: F3-10.
117 Webb & Wright IV: 376, V: 87; Hammond-Tooke 1974: 112.
118 Derek Berliner, 'Sad,bad, mad idea for EC', *Daily Dispatch*, 28 March 2015; Hugo Canham, 'A morning of devastation', *City Press*, 15 February 2015.
119 *City Press*, 15 February 2015; Andrew Donaldson, 'Dagga madness', www.politicsweb.co.za, accessed 14 March 2015.
120 Paterson 2009: 3.
121 Paterson 2009: 3–4.
122 See chapter 4.
123 Booth 2003: 339.
124 Ian Birrell, 'War against drugs just not working', *Sunday Times*, 3 May 2015.
125 *Legalbrief*, 8 July 2014.
126 'Grow your own marijuana policy', *Mail & Guardian*, 30 May 2014. For a clear and concise discussion of the failed war on drugs and issues of decriminalisation, see Parry 2002 and Parry & Myers 2011.
127 www.news24.com, accessed 20 June 2014; see also *Legalbrief*, 20 June 2014: 'Woman seeks release to attend to injured goat'.
128 Williams, who suffered from depression, took his own life in 2014.
129 Vedic scripts, as mentioned above, associated the drug with the benevolence and worship of Lord Shiva (Du Toit 1996: 128).
130 Booth 2003: 316; Davis & Simon: 63–4.
131 *Prince v President of the Law Society and Others* 2002(2) SA 794 (CC).
132 'He might be liberal, but this Pope doesn't dig dope', *Weekend Post*, 21 June 2014.
133 See Kahn 1972: 106; Bensusan 1972: 116.
134 Booth 2003: 24.
135 Translated into Arabic and other languages, it was widely available to scholars and served as an essential medical text until well into the seventeenth century (Booth 2003: 31, 48, 70).
136 Castle & Murray 2004: 2; Booth 2003: 23; Paterson 2009: 19, 20. Although dagga heightens the senses and can enhance sexual physicality, it is not, in fact, an aphrodisiac.
137 Booth 2003: 109.
138 Kahn 1972: 114; Hoctor *et al.*: F3-10; Booth 2003: 55.
139 Pers. comm., 8 December 2014.

140 'Karoo state of mind', *Sunday Times*, 14 September 2014.

141 Solowij 1999: 41; Booth 2003: 6, 349.

142 Booth 2003: 71.

143 Castle & Murray 2004: 45.

144 Le Couteur & Burreson 2004: 130; 'Harmless, harmful or medicinal?', *Mail & Guardian*, 4 July 2014.

145 Kahn 1972: 111; Hoctor *et al.*: F3-10.

146 'Secure Italian military lab to grow medicinal marijuana', Steve Shearer, 18 September 2014, www.reuters.com; 'Italian army takes high road with marijuana', Steve Sherer, *Daily Dispatch*, 12 October 2014.

147 Parry & Myers, 2014: 400.

148 'Medical dagga trials urged', Estelle Ellis, *The Herald*, 30 May 2014; Parry & Myers 2014: 400.

149 www.southafrica.info, accessed 30 June 2014.

150 www.allAfrica.com, accessed 30 June 2014.

151 'A campaign against pain', *Sunday Times*, 24 August 2014.

152 *Legalbrief*, 18 September 2014. The Medical Innovation Bill was re-introduced in Parliament on 9 September 2014 by the late Ambrosini's colleague, Narend Singh of the Inkatha Freedom Party (Antony Mitchell, IFP Chief of Staff, pers. comm., 17 February 2015). Since then, the DA's stance appears to have softened somewhat. In a recent interview, the party's leader, Mmusi Maimane, noted that *should* dagga be legalised, 'access must be conditional', its medical use regulated, and production restricted to 'a managed environment, so that not everyone can grow and distribute the weed' (*Sunday Times*, 3 May 2015).

153 www.mrc.co.za/media/2015; 'MPs huff and puff over dagga legislation', Babalo Ndenze, *The Herald*, 28 May 2015.

154 Charles Parry, pers. comm., 2 June 2015.

155 'Dagga's appeal to daring investors', *Weekend Post*, 21 June 2014.

156 Julian Stobbs, International Crime Stoppers Conference, *Legalbrief*, 14 October 2014; see also Parry 2002: 296–7.

157 'New Bob Marley marijuana gon' make you feel irie', *Mail & Guardian*, 21 November 2014.

158 After Mazikana *et al.*: 119.

159 Booth 2003: 2.

160 Booth 2003: 27.

161 Booth 2003: 27–8; Douglas 1979: 39. The one through whom the voice of God spoke, was known as *messiah*, or 'the anointed one'. For more on Old Testament 'messianism', see Douglas 1979: 811–813.

162 Douglas 1979: 606; Booth 2003: 28.

163 Douglas 1979: 39.

164 Mills 2003: 41.

165 Booth 2003: 113; Mills 2003: 40.
166 Mills 2003: 39, 45, 46.
167 Mills 2003: 69; Booth 2003: 112–4.
168 Booth 2003: 113, 121. This is not entirely true, since the fastest method of delivering cannabinoids is by smoking dagga and, like smoking tobacco, smoking dagga over a long term can be harmful to one's health. Cannabinoids can, however, be ingested by other methods, including oil, pills or vapourisers (see Parry & Myers 2014: 399).
169 Booth 2003: 119.
170 Booth 2003: 142.
171 Booth 2003: 142; Mills 2003: 3, 67, 157.
172 Mills 2003: 160–1.
173 Booth 2003: 143; Mills 2003: 6, 183.
174 Booth 2003: 224–5.
175 Mills 2003: 179–87, 190–1.
176 Mills 2003: 219.
177 Booth 2003: 394.
178 McPhee: 92.

Select bibliography

Abbreviations:

NADA: *The Southern Rhodesian Native Affairs Department Annual*, Salisbury, Rhodesia.

RSEA: *Records of South Eastern Africa*, Nine volumes, edited by G. McC Theal (Cape Town: Struik Facsimile Reprint, 1964).

SALJ: *South African Law Journal*

SAMJ: *South African Medical Journal*

Abraham, D.P.: 'The Monomotapa Dynasty', *NADA*, 36 (1959), pp. 59–84.

Alberti, Ludwig: *Account of ... the Xhosa in 1807* (Cape Town: A.A. Balkema, 1968).

Axelson, Eric: *Vasco da Gama: The Diary of his Travels through African Waters 1497–1499* (Somerset West: Stephan Phillips, 1998).

Bain, Andrew Geddes: *Journals of Andrew Geddes Bain* (1826). Edited by Margaret Hermina Lister (Cape Town: Van Riebeeck Society, 1949).

Bensusan, A.D.: 'The Use and Effects of Dagga in South Africa – A Medical Assessment', *SALJ*, 89 (1972), pp. 116–123.

Booth, Martin: *Cannabis, a History* (New York: Picador, 2003).

Burchell, William J.: *Travels in the Interior of Southern Africa*. Two volumes (London: Longman, Hurst, Rees & Orme, 1822 & 1824).

Castle, David & Robin Murray (eds.): *Marijuana and Madness* (New York: Cambridge University Press, 2004).

Caton-Thompson, G. *The Zimbabwe Culture: Ruins and Reactions* (Oxford: Clarendon Press, 1931).

Crampton, Hazel, Jeff Peires & Carl Vernon (eds.): *Into the Hitherto Unknown: Ensign Beutler's Expedition to the Eastern Cape, 1752* (Cape Town: Van Riebeeck Society, 2013).

Crampton, Hazel: *The Side of the Sun at Noon* (Johannesburg: Jacana Media, 2014).

Dapper, Dr O.: 'Kaffaria or Land of the Kafirs, also named Hottentots' (1668), *The Early Cape Hottentots*. Edited by I. Schapera and B. Farrington (Cape Town: Van Riebeeck Society, 1933).

Davis, Stephen & Peter Simon: *Reggae International* (London: Thames and Hudson, 1983).

De Grevenbroek, Johannes G.: 'An Elegant and Accurate Account of the African Race Living Round the Cape of Good Hope commonly called Hottentots' (1695), *The Early Cape Hottentots*.

Edited by I. Schapera and B. Farrington (Cape Town: Van Riebeeck Society, 1933).

Dos Santos, Frair Joao, 'Ethiopia Oriental', *RSEA*, vol. VII (1609), pp. 183–370.

Douglas, J.D. (ed.): *The New Bible Dictionary* (Michigan: Eerdmans, 1979).

Du Toit, Brian M.: 'Pot by any other name is still ... A study of the diffusion of cannabis', *South African Journal of Ethnology*, 19 (1996), pp. 127–135.

Gardner, Helen (ed.): *The New Oxford Book of English Verse* (Oxford: Clarendon Press, 1973).

Godée-Molsbergen, Dr E.C.: *Reizen in Zuid-Afrika in de Hollandse Tijd* ...Volume III ('S-Gravenhage: Martinus Nijhoff, 1922).

Gordon, Robert Jacob: *Cape travels, 1777–1786.* Two volumes, edited by Peter E. Raper & Maurice Boucher (Johannesburg: Brenthurst Press, 1988).

Hammond-Tooke, W.D. (ed.): *The Bantu-speaking Peoples of Southern Africa* (London & Boston: Routledge/Kegan Paul, 1974).

Hill, Harry: *Bumper Book of Bloopers* (London: Faber & Faber, 2011).

Hoctor, S.V., M.G. Cowling & J.R.L. Milton (eds.): *South African Criminal Law and Procedure, Volume III: Statutory Offences* (Cape Town: Juta, 1988, Service No. 17, 2007).

Jarski, Rosemarie: *The funniest thing you never said* II (London: Ebury Press, 2010).

Jarski, Rosemarie: *The funniest thing you never said*

(London: Ebury Press, 2004).

Junod, Henri A.: *The Life of a South African Tribe.* Two volumes (Neuchatel: Imprimerie Attinger Fréres, 1912).

Juta's Statutes of South Africa, 2012/2013, Volume 1 (Cape Town: Juta & Co., 2013).

Kahn, Ellison: 'Recent Legislation', *SALJ*, 89 (1972), pp. 105–115.

Klatzow, David: *Justice Denied* (Cape Town: Zebra Press, 2014).

Kolbe, Peter: *The Present State of the Cape of Good-Hope.* Two volumes (London: W. Innys, 1731).

Krige, E. Jensen & J.D. Krige: *The Realm of a Rain-Queen* (Oxford: Oxford University Press, 1956).

Laidler, P. W.: 'The Magic Medicine of the Hottentots', *South African Journal of Science*, Volume 25 (December 1928), pp. 433–447.

Le Couteur, Penny & Jay Burreson: *Napoleon's Buttons: 17 Molecules that Changed History* (New York: Tarcher/Penguin, 2004).

Leibbrandt, H.C.: *Precis of the Archives of Cape of Good Hope. Letters Despatched 1652–1662.* Three volumes (Cape Town: Government Printers, 1900).

Lloyd, John & John Mitchinson: *The QI Book of the Dead* (London: Faber & Faber, 2009).

Maclennan, Ben: *Apartheid: The Lighter Side* (Cape Town: Chameleon Press, 1990).

Manson, Andrew: 'The Shashe-Limpopo Basin and the Origin of the Zimbabwe Culture; People of the

Second Millennium', *New History of South Africa*. Edited by Herman Giliomee & Bernard Mbenga (Cape Town: Tafelberg, 2007).

Mazikana, P.C., I.J. Johnstone & R.G.S. Douglas: *Zimbabwe Epic* (Harare: National Archives, 1984).

McPhee, Nancy: *The Bumper Book of Insults* (London: Chancellor Press, 1981).

Mentzel, O.F.: *A Complete and Authentic Geographical and Topographical Description of the Famous and (all things considered) Remarkable African Cape of Good Hope* (1785–7). Three volumes, edited by H.J. Mandelbrote (Cape Town: Van Riebeeck Society, 1921, 1925 & 1944).

Mills, James H.: *Cannabis Britannica: Empire, Trade, and Prohibition 1800–1928* (New York: Oxford University Press, 2003).

Mossop, Dr E.E. (ed.): *The Journals of Brink and Rhenius* (Cape Town: Van Riebeeck Society, 1947).

Nienaber, G.S. & P.E. Raper: *Hottentot (Khoekhoen) Place Names* (Pretoria: Human Sciences Research Ccouncil, 1983).

Owen, Captain: 'The Bay of Delagoa' (1823), *RSEA* II. Cape Town, 1964.

Parry, C.D.H. & B.J. Meyers: 'Legalising Medical Use of Cannabis in South Africa: Is the Empirical Evidence Sufficient to Support Policy Shifts in this Direction?' *SAMJ*, Volume 104, 6 (June 2014), pp. 399–400.

Parry, Charles & Bronwyn Myers: 'Beyond the

Rhetoric: Towards a More Effective and Humane Drug Policy Framework in South Africa', *SAMJ*, vol. 101, 10 (2011), pp. 704–6.

Parry, Charles: 'Critical Issues in the Debate on Decriminalization or Legislation of Cannabis in South Africa', *SAMJ*, vol. 92, 9, (2002), pp. 696–697.

Paterson, Craig: 'Prohibition & Resistance: A Socio-political Exploration of the Changing Dynamics of the Southern African Cannabis Trade, c. 1850–the present' (Master of Arts dissertation, Rhodes University, Grahamstown, 2009).

Raven-Hart, R.: *Before Van Riebeeck* (Cape Town: Struik, 1967).

Rosenthal, Eric: *Encyclopaedia of Southern Africa* (London: Frederick Warne & Co., 1973).

Saugestad, Sidsel: '"When I say Land I Talk about my Mother": Contemporary Perspectives on Indigenous Organisations and Encounters in Southern Africa', *The Khoisan Identities & Cultural Heritage Conference* (Cape Town: Infosource, 1998).

Sherrin, Ned: *Oxford Dictionary of Humorous Quotations* (Oxford: Oxford University Press, 1996).

Smith, Andrew: *The Diary of Dr Andrew Smith, Director of the 'Expedition for Exploring Central Africa' 1834–6.* Two volumes, edited by Percival R. Kirby (Cape Town: Van Riebeeck Society, 1939–40).

Smith, C.A.: *Common names of South African Plants.*

Botanical Research Institute; Botanical Survey Memoir, 35 (Pretoria: Government Printer, 1966).

Solowij, Nadia: *Cannabis and Cognitive Functioning* (Cambridge University Press, 1999).

Somerville, Dr William: *William Somerville's Narrative of his Journeys to the Eastern Cape Frontier and to Lattakoe 1799–1802*. Edited by Edna and Frank Bradlow (Cape Town: Van Riebeeck Society, 1979).

South African Criminal Law Reports (Cape Town: Juta & Co., 1999).

South African Law Reports, March–April 2002 (Cape Town: Juta & Co., 2002).

Ten Rhyne, William: 'An Account of the Cape of Good Hope and the Hottentotes, the Natives of that Country' (1686), *A Collection of Voyages and Travels*, IV. Edited by Lintot and Osborn. (London: 1745).

Thompson, George: *Travels and Adventures in Southern Africa* (1827). Two volumes, edited by Vernon S. Forbes (Cape Town: Van Riebeek Society, 1968).

Valentyn, Francois: *Description of the Cape of Good Hope with the matters concerning it...* (1726). Two volumes, edited by Dr E.H. Rait, & translated by Maj. R. Raven-Hart (Cape Town: Van Riebeeck Society, 1973).

Van Riebeeck, Jan: *The Journal of Jan van Riebeeck*. Three volumes, edited by H.B. Thom (Cape Town, Amsterdam: Van Riebeeck Society & A.A.

Balkema, 1958).

Voigt, E.A.: *Mapungubwe: An Archaeozoological Interpretation of an Iron Age Community* (Pretoria: Transvaal Museum Monograph, 1983).

Webb, C. de B., & J.B. Wright (eds.): *The James Stuart Archive*. Five volumes (Pietermaritzburg: University of Natal Press, 1976–2001).

White, William: *Journal of a Voyage performed in the Lion extra Indiaman, from Madras to Columbo, and Da Lagoa Bay, on the eastern coast of Africa; (where the ship was condemned) in the year 1798. With some manners and customs of the inhabitants of Da Lagoa Bay, and a vocabulary of the language.* (London: John Stockdale, 1800).

Wild, Antony: *Coffee: A Dark History* (New York: Norton & Co., 2004).

Williams, Donovan (ed.): *The Journal and Selected Writings of the Reverend Tiyo Soga* (Cape Town: A.A. Balema, 1983).

Cape Archives, Roeland Street, Cape Town:
ACC 612 (34).